SELL MORE BOOKS AT LIVE EVENTS:

HOW TO SELL MORE BOOKS AT CONVENTIONS, SHOWS, SIGNINGS, EVENTS, AND BEYOND!

Christopher D. Schmitz

Christopher D. Schmitz

PUBLISHED BY TREESHAKER BOOKS
please visit:
http://www.authorchristopherdschmitz.com

Contents

Christopher D. Schmitz

Chapter One: Why This book?

Introduction

Maybe you're like me. Perhaps you've written a book and been able to sell it to folks face-to-face, but maybe you've failed to really harness the power of ye olde interwebs, (be it from a Luddite inclination or a simple inability to succeed at the whole selling online thing.) I know the latter is true in my case.

Or maybe you make a ton of sales on Amazon, B&N, Kobo, iBooks, etc., but you want to learn how to sell books face-to-face and add that sales channel to your business. Either way, this book will help you.

Here's me: I sell really well in person, less so online. I think my books are great. People who read them honestly like them (even when asked what they really think and after being given explicit permission to be honest ... well, not *everybody*. There are a few one-star reviews, but fewer of them after releasing a short story about an author who kidnapped a nasty book review troll and going in reverse - *Misery*, but I digress.) The point is that my skill set lends me to selling very well in face-to-ace, physical situations. Trying to do the same through a computer screen has stripped me of my biggest asset: me.

I'm not particularly skilled. Or handsome. Or charismatic (I suddenly need a hug and a Hallmark card,) but I have something a lot of traditional "salespeople" don't. I care about other humans. I value their experience, their personal story. I also have enough know-how to quickly move someone from setting a hook with a quick pitch to closing the sale.

Here's the good news: that last part is something that can be taught.

Maybe you're like me. Then again, maybe you're *not* like me. Maybe the thought of talking to another live human to make a sale makes you cringe like you just cannon-balled into a frigid pool. That's okay. I've got tips for you, too, so remember to plug your nose as you hit the water and keep reading.

After encountering more than a few authors, and even other artist/creators at similar vending opportunities and being asked if they could sit awhile and watch my process or pick my brain, I decided there was the need for a book regarding my particular set of skills. I'm always happy to help and firmly believe in the motto of the 20Booksto50K group (an online author collective that I participate in) that a rising tide lifts all ships. I am more than happy to help and have taught several folks how to sell better, how to maximize their sales, or best prepare themselves for selling books at live events. (And technically, most of the principles in this book could be used to help you sell pretty much any product.)

Regardless of your particular personality, you probably want to sell as many books as possible when you book a live event. Just as I've taught many authors previously, and in person, this book will teach you the same things.

There are many types of live events to consider. The list includes:

Book festivals
Library events
Book signings
Meet and greets
Conventions
Trade shows
Craft fairs
Flea markets
and on and on…

The point is this: there is a market for everything and a convention or trade show for even the most unseemly things (I kid you not, there's even professional trade shows and conventions for workers of the adult film industry where I imagine a guy could shake Ron Jeremy's hand and then immediately need a scalding hot shower.) I taught a library workshop during the last NaNoWriMo where I worked with an older, retired woman to brainstorm marketing ideas for her coleslaw-only cook book. We thought up a dozen ways she could get her final product into people's hands. There's a niche for just about anything.

Maybe now you're stuck thinking about a romantic comedy featuring Ron Jeremy and his coleslaw restaurant. That's how the mind works. We get stuck in a tunnel and can't get past our own thoughts, and that's why it's good to find content or partners that can spark ideas.

That's what this book is. Tinder to start a flame which will help you sell more books. If it's not enough, I am available to consult and welcome authors who contact me through my blog or website: authorchristopherdschmitz.com.

Also, I call dibs on the Ron Jeremy Coleslaw idea. That one sounds like a real wiener. I mean winner.

About Me

I remember being a cub scout as a child. I was pretty young, but I vividly recall winning a contest to sell buttons. It was a town-wide thing, but it was a small town. Hallmark Christmas movie small. But I distinctly remember that, opposed to a product scouts usually sell like Christmas trees or popcorn, the button didn't really do anything. There was no real purpose. I mean, why would anyone want this thing?

It didn't matter. I wanted to win, and so win I did—and I scored a Walkman in the mid-1980s (cue whatever MCU Starlord meme you find appropriate). It wasn't that a silly button had any intrinsic value—the reason I sold so many (literally, I sold something like 1 button for 25% of the entire town's population,) was that I went where people were and I asked them to buy one.

Sales aren't quite as easy as just showing up and asking … but almost. If you don't 1) find an audience, and 2) make the ask, then nothing else matters. Those leg-breaking mobsters, I mean Girl Scouts, have figured this out with cookie sales. I've seen them at malls, sitting in front of doorways, and even getting tables at the same places and events I often go to and sell my books.

But this was supposed to be about me selling books. Well, I'm no girl scout. They don't have a sash in my size, but they did give me a nice restraining order. All jokes aside, they are just one of many examples that a DIY seller ought to look at and learn from.

I had a few sales jobs through college. After graduation, I swung a hammer as a carpenter for a while, a trade I learned growing up, and then talked my way into a real estate office gig and became the top sales agent in the office within a few months. Right as the real estate bubble was bursting in the mid-aughts, I sold my own home sight-unseen for full asking price while I moved into fulltime nonprofit work and wound up in North Dakota.

They weren't joking. There wasn't much profit in nonprofits, but it was satisfying to work with people. I heard their stories. I broke bread with people. I encouraged folks and hugged them when they cried.

After a few years, I had a shift during all the tumult in the North Dakota oil craziness (I was in the middle of it in Williston, ND where a reasonable place to live suddenly went bananas, when housing prices went from affordable to suddenly being the most expensive per capita housing costs in the whole of the USA. But it was the gunfire in what had previously been the nicest part of town when I was walking with my kids that told me the time had come to move.)

As I write this, I've only just stepped away from training my replacement after a ten-year career working with teens at Youth for Christ (YFC). But in between Williston and that, I worked for a company pitching their product to consumers across the nation. I won't name drop them, but they invest a lot of time studying the psychology of salesmanship and it is a very high pressure, rapid-fire pitching, constant rejection kind of job. But the cost of entry was high on their items. A book? Far more reasonable. I got a lot of great experience with them, both in pitch-work and on how to keep costs low while traveling, and it still raises eyebrows when folks learn that I worked for them.

My time with YFC also taught me something vitally important: the importance of relationships. You might or might not have any sort of faith-based framework. But you could be an atheist and still utilize this big takeaway. *Relationships are everything.* YFC has a way of thinking about relationship building that revolutionized the way I think about things; it's a model called 3Story®.

The 3Story® framework is simple and I'll break it down without getting preachy. Think of a Venn diagram with three interlocking circles.

One of those circles represents *your story*. Another represents the larger story, *God's story* (which anyone working for YFC would have an intersection with on their own, already.) Our goal is to build relationships with teens, interlocking our story with theirs and then, as appropriate, show them how that circle interlocking with ours helps us live fulfilled and empowered lives of meaning and purpose, and then show them how to intersect *their story* with God's story.

In sales, you have a story as the vendor, including your personality, mood, disposition, etc. Your customer has their story as well, including all the distractions of family, cell phones, budget, personal concerns and baggage. Your desire is to intersect your circle with theirs and move that larger circle, your product (in this case, a book) into their sphere. Show how it is relevant, meets a need, appeals to common interest, and the like.

I'm very good at intersecting my circle with others. And that's why I'm not a great digital marketer. Most of mine are soft skills and they come down to nuance and tone. It's not just in what's said, but also in what's left unsaid. Being good at sales is a lot like being a minister. There's an old adage for public speakers that goes, "They won't remember what you said, but they'll remember how you made them feel."

And that's true in sales.

Here's what sales really is: building relationships. One of the biggest tools in your box of sales tricks is the fact that a buyer gets to meet the author. That adds huge intrinsic value and, in this day and age of information traveling at the speed of a mouse and keyboard, consumers want to keep in touch with the author.

That brings me to my next point: the continued author/reader relationship is critical. It could be the topic of an entire extra book, but I'm trying to keep this one succinct.

You might throw this whole book away right now and you'll still get something of value if *you take to heart the next paragraph.*

I teach many workshops, panels, and conferences, and I consult regularly on books for authors. I have two books I *always* recommend. The first book is The Indie Author's Bible (and I only say that because I wrote it and have a horse in this race.) The second is Newsletter Ninja by Tammi Labrecque. It's easy, informative, and my biggest regret is not sticking with my newsletter early on and came into it only after releasing several books. My mailing list has been pivotal to me retaining and communicating with readers, and it's a far better tool than any social media platform. Her book might be the best investment of less than $20 that you can make in your author knowledge base (aside from the Indie Author's Bible, that is.)

And I'll repeat myself here: if you need someone to consult on a book idea or project, feel free to reach out to me through my Inside the Inkwell blog or via my website.

Also, I don't know Tammi Labrecque. We've never met. But her book helped me get a grasp on the whole newsletter thing—and not just the *how to* part, but also the *why*. Other writers have helped teach me through their books, and that is why I focus so much time on paying it forward. We share and we teach each other.

I'll say it again: a rising tide lifts all ships—and that relationship thing isn't just for your readers. It's also important to build relationships with other authors.

Relationships

I hinted at it earlier, but relationships, when selling to customers, connects their need with an answer. It's a lot like writing in that way. Nonfiction books are written to answer a question and meet the needs of a reader; you didn't pick up this book looking to find out about formatting paperbacks.

Once you can find out what a person wants or hopes to gain from a book, you can help to meet his or her needs. You, and your books, exist to meet a need that someone else has.

When you really internalize this concept, you'll have no problem helping someone, even if they aren't the best fit for your book. For example, if you get a book signing at a local bookstore or chain and don't have a crowd who is going to show up to see you, make sure you honor that store's time by being of service. Meet customers. Say hello. Offer to share about your books, but if you're doing a signing at a Barnes and Noble for your erotic space adventure and someone tells you they only read true crime, point them to *Killing Lincoln* or similar books. Definitely mention who you are and why you're there but being helpful and graceful when talking with someone who is clearly outside your target market will earn you karma points. You can't spend them on anything, but it's a good general practice to be helpful whenever you can.

And isn't that how we really ought to live, anyway? We should always be looking to help other people if we can. That's part of being a decent human being. I can't say that I always live up to this; human nature is not defined as a tendency to do the right and moral thing—quite the opposite, actually. But if we can leave the people we meet a little better for having engaged them, then that counts as a win. It might not sell books, but I'd rather be a good person than a rich one. And sometimes it *does* pay off. I've actually had customers tell me what they are most interested in reading and then sent them to buy books from other authors who I knew would be a perfect fit (*remember that part about relationships with other authors?*) Some have them come back so happy that they bought my books as gifts for other people in the end.

On another occasion, I chatted with a lady who turned out to be a booker for a cable access show, and that turned into an interview in a nearby city. That, in turn, produced a feature on another, regional television show. Immediate sales are nice, but they are often just one leg of a stool that is your author platform.

Fair warning: while there are other highly valuable outcomes aside from selling that come from live events, do not use looking for them as an excuse to *not* ask for the sale. Many people will not purchase something on a cold sale *unless you ask them to*. In the sales and author spheres, we call this the Call to Action or CTA. Want them to join your newsletter? You usually have to ask. Want them to click a link? Ask. Buy the next in your series? Pump up that CTA. Your success rates will improve dramatically.

I know that some people are very averse to relationship stuff. The classic archetype of the reclusive author holed up alone in a wooded, secluded cabin with nothing to keep him company but a typewriter and a bottle of scotch still exists. Heck, it still dominates Hollywood as a romantic notion. But that image needs to die; it is the exception and not the rule. I don't teach authors I consult for to be exceptions—it's too difficult to find success running around in the rain and hoping lightning will strike. You'll just end up cold and wet. Here's what I mean: you won't find a real modicum of success by hiding in the back. If you want book sales, you've got to go out and get them. Shake your own trees: it's the thought behind my publishing company, TreeShaker Books. We only work with authors who are willing to go out and make their own noise ... nobody else will care about your book like you do—so make some damn noise about it.

Introverts, you may have a hard time with this. But it's as simple as playing pretend, or acting.

While introverts deplete their energy with outward, engaging activities with people outside their bubble, you can learn to fake it for a few hours or through a couple of days selling at events. You'll sleep hard to recharge, but equipped with the tools in this book, you'll make more sales. Just think of it more like showing up to a job ... and believe me, live events will be work.

And never fear. There are shortcuts you can take to help make immediate connections with people you've only just met. It'll also make *you* feel a little like Sherlock Holmes, and it'll make *those* people feel like you have connected more deeply with them or like you've known them longer than a couple of minutes. The trick is, like Holmes, you've got to make some assumptions about a person based on the scant information you get at a glance.

There are several ways we can draw the necessary conclusions. You can often make an educated guess about what someone likes based on their appearance. Most humans consciously dress themselves, so a T-shirt advertising their favorite band or movie might tell you something about music preferences or fandoms; likewise, if it is a shirt worn by the local library volunteers. Does it have a logo, TV graphic, or movie characters that will help you can connect with them?

Here's an example. Say you're standing in the front at Barnes and Noble to sign books for your indie post-apocalyptic thriller and a young person walks in wearing a leather vest with a Wings graphic on the back. You could easily assume they are a fan of Darryl from *Walking Dead* and would be a perfect fit for your book. "Hey, I love your vest. Did you see that last episode?" Recognizing someone else's fandom honors them at a deep level. And when you share a fandom at any level, it builds an immediate bridge.

Not everything is T-shirt graphics. Sometimes there are other factors, too. You could assume that someone in a MAGA cap is a bad fit for your nonfiction book that casts a feminist manifesto while someone in a pink pussy hat would be an ideal reader. That doesn't mean you can't talk to the nice lady in the MAGA gear. Honey catches flies better than vinegar, says the old proverb, and it's not going to pain you to be nice or helpful to someone with wildly opposite beliefs, no matter what CNN or FoxNews tell you. *Just be nice.*

Remember, as much as it is up to you, always decide to be a decent human.

These shortcuts *can get you into trouble* if you don't use them responsibly. So, heed a little caution before using them. We want to *draw conclusions* and not *jump to conclusions*. You might meet a guy wearing an AC/DC concert tour shirt, but he's borrowing it or wearing it ironically and he hates rock music. Perhaps you're booked at a literary festival in a county that has a reputation for liking certain genre books, but the person in front of you might *hate* those genres. I was talking with someone who said he loved sci-fi and compared an element in one of my books to a beloved piece from Star Wars, and he says, "I *hate* Star Wars." (Not just hate for one of the trilogies or films—but the whole franchise.)

Drawing too deep an assumption can get you into big trouble. The bigger the importance of that assumption, the greater the danger. Don't make an assumption about an Asian's math skills or a black person's love for rap or hip hop. Having trouble ascertaining a gender … maybe just leave it alone, ask their name, and use that … gender is not important to telling them about your books. And don't ever, *I mean ever*, ask the lady with the belly when she is due … dental work is expensive.

Chapter Two: Every Event is Different

Types of Events

What kind of book events should you do? There are many kinds of events out there and I've already mentioned book festivals, library events, book signings, meet and greets, conventions, trade shows, craft fairs, and flea markets. You could add to that list things like guest appearances at book clubs, writing or arts workshops, holiday festivals, lunch and learns, street festivals, and community celebrations. Almost anything can become bookish if you interest the promoters in pursuing a literary bent. Pre-COVID, my area had a local circuit for some events called Pop-Up Bookstore and Books & Beer that toured a few weekends every other month or so at regional breweries.

Every event is going to have its own unique angle and will attract its own kind of audience. That, along with the dynamics of any individual show, should ultimately help you decide if it's good for you. If the show is difficult to be at for you, it won't be a good fit, even if there is a good/receptive audience. For example, if you are recently sober and struggling to stay clean, the Books & Beer at a brewery is likely a terrible choice for you to attend.

I'm going to insert a break right here to differentiate between live event types. The rest of the book will primarily discuss vending from a table or booth when you are surrounded by other vendors, artists, and creators doing the same thing (selling) with their products. This is fundamentally different from an event appearance, book signing, or the like. For example, you might be a keynote speaker at a mental health workers' convention and have a small table set up in the back to earn extra dollars from people interested in your content and experiences. The same goes for a traveling preacher or evangelist where you have a merchandise table set up in the narthex or back of the church where people can pick up your books and materials.

At these events, your sales booth is secondary to your purpose in coming. Many speakers and business professionals are encouraged by so-called experts to write a book to add a level of authority to their presentations, give their audience more, remind them of your topic/content, or make a few extra dollars. I'm not saying there is anything wrong with this and it is a valid model.

The speaker model is a slightly different model and I want to bring up that fact. The difference is that you become a known figure in that market. You're the *big show*. If this was a big church event and you were a guest speaker, everyone there knows your name and what you're about—every person attending is a "warm sale." They may be specifically looking to buy from you during or after the event. In the vendor model we talk about in this book, your sales funnel begins from a cold start and likely with no familiarity with you or your books.

Ultimately, this book will give you valuable tools and principles for both models, but it focuses on the sales table as the priority. When I do events, my main focus is on the sales booth. I will often book speaking appearances during a convention as a panelist, workshop teacher, or guest appearance, but those are all done in the hope that people will visit my table afterward and make a purchase, whereas the inverse is typically true in the other kinds of events: your appearance is the important part and book sales are tertiary.

Because every event will be significantly different, I will focus on principles that are transitive. Despite the nuances, there will be many aspects of live events that will remain the same across the board. At least in generic terms, the book's principles will apply, though it will be up to you to ferret out specific differences as appropriate to your genre, your audience, and specific events. However, I will give you specific examples with stories unique to me or my circle of author friends.

Ideally, it's nice to have plenty of information on any show before attending. If possible, I like to go to a show beforehand—especially the larger ones, but that's not always possible. A lot of events might be new and so organizers don't have a lot of data yet, or maybe it's a larger convention with high fees for attendees and that makes a first-hand experience cost prohibitive for you.

Luckily, many websites exist to help vendors network and share experiences. They might give you feedback about which shows are their favorites and the ones of which you should be wary.

Area shows like craft festivals, vendor markets, maker fairs, and smaller shows are a little easier to get first-hand knowledge. You likely have someone in your circle who has experience with it (even as an attendee) if it's close and if it's cheap or free. But you can't always get an expectation set for every show and shouldn't let that be a hang-up that prevents you from getting out there and selling. Once you learn the basic gist of a *type* of show, everything else will come together and then it's just a matter of balancing a budget against your expected income from a show.

In my first few years, I did not aim to make big profits, not until I had several different books out that I could pitch to readers. A reader might dislike one kind of book, but love another. But we'll discuss that more later. One of the things I was doing, besides learning how to improve my sales skills, was learning the flow of event selling and realizing my potential. Essentially, I was gathering data.

After finding my stride, I realized that I sold a pretty consistent number of books based on the percentage of people through the door. After tracking data for several years, I realized that number was between 0.5 and 1 percent. I tweaked and improved and now I sell a book to between one and three percent at cons up to 25,000 people and 0.5-1 percent at larger conventions. If there are 50,000 attendees and if I can set up the way I prefer to maximize what I'm doing, I expect to sell about 300-500 books.

My audience is SFF readers of a broad scope. I write several series including Urban Fantasy, Space Opera, High Fantasy, Military SF, Horror, and a niched Police Comedy. Of course, I also do nonfiction which typically sells itself. When someone is interested in my books on author stuff, they let you know.

Once I determine whether an event is a good fit for me, I try to crunch some numbers. That means knowing a few things about the event or making an educated guess. I often ask organizers these questions directly, but many will not give you trustworthy answers (they're selling table spaces after all and may fudge them a little.)

I ask about the attendance in prior years and expectations for the upcoming event. I want to know if there is free parking, the table or booth size, and whether I can choose my placement. Most events include a table and chairs, but at some you must bring your own—and that information is vital. If you don't have your own Wi-Fi hotspot, you may need to ask about internet access (I bring my own just in case) and it's handy to know about power access, though I always plan to bring a charger pack in case I need it. Is there an entry fee for attendees, and if so, how many tickets do I get for my booth helpers—if I need more, is there a discount vendor rate for additional tickets?

For many of the events that I do, I have the option of being either an artist/creator or a vendor. Vendors pay more, but generally have a nicer space and are allowed to resell items as a whole-seller; some events will allow crafters, artists, and the like to pay a cheaper rate but they can only sell their own items. While this is generally the best option, it isn't always. Also, is this only a vendor/sales event only, or are there additional aspects to the event, such as workshops, panels, or speaking opportunities you could be a part of?

That last question, along with many others, can usually be answered by looking at the event's online information. You'll plan differently according to the answers.

Live convention events are great because of the mindset of the attendees. When they walk into an area called the "Vendor Hall" they have already psychologically conditioned themselves to spend money. Sure, they may be browsing when they walk past, but they know that whatever they see inside there will require a transaction.

You will also want to know how far away the event is to travel, and what is your *best* lodging option if there is an overnight stay. Best isn't always the cheapest, but usually it is, for the sake of your bottom line. You may want to double up with a family vacation and use the trip as a business write off by spending a day or two at a show and then relaxing with the kids. If you do that, staying at the Itchy-Blanket Roach Motel might be out of the question. I've *usually* found that staying with the designated hotel partners is the worst option for conventions unless the event is paying for your stay. Also, in my early days, I doubled up with a lot of other vendors and would rent an Airbnb or split a hotel room which vastly reduced my overhead. I still do this occasionally, but I often need the extra space for my booth helper(s) to sleep.

Figuring out your travel costs is important. You can mitigate food expense by bringing along a cooler.

The info I really want to know is what kind of visibility will I have and how many people will see me? I need an estimated head count to do some math … and you thought you could get away from arithmetic by becoming a writer?

At smaller shows under 3,000 attendees, I generally sell very well and will sell a book to about 3% in attendance. That number actually decreases as it gets higher, and I'll explain the reasons for that. But at shows between 1,000 to 1,500, my number is more like 6% and sometimes higher. In that attendance range, I generally sell 65-85 books. Let's call that a Tier 3 show with 1,000-1,500 people being Tier 3B and 1,500-3,000 being Tier 3A. I sell a book to 2-3% at Tier 3A. Anything smaller than Tier 3, we'll call Tier 4, and I generally sell about 35 books at any show under 1,000 attendees.

Let's call Tier 2 the 5,000 to 20,000 range. I know that leaves some gaps in the numbers, but I'm a writer, not a mathematician, and the edges of these shows are always a little spongy anyway. I usually sell one book per one to one-half percent at these, with that number going down as the attendance increases. These shows are typically about 200 book sale shows for me.

Tier 1 are large shows, usually 40,000-100,000 attendees. I can usually do about 0.3% to a little higher than a half percent at shows this size. That would mean a high-water mark at around 600 units. To hit those kinds of numbers, you will need additional help and visibility, meaning much higher costs. It may mean additional booth spaces or tables which would double your event cost, and those sorts of shows are crazy-wild; everyone is there to spend or vend. It might include shows like San Diego Comic Convention, GenCon Gaming Convention, E3 expo, the Great American Outdoor Show, and others, each being among the largest event types catering to their audience. They take on a carnival-like atmosphere and feel almost like a coke-fueled tour of Disneyland.

Cocaine or not, you can't get through all of Disney in a single weekend. You also can't get anything to eat on a limited budget or rent a room for a reasonable rate. It's a production to get in and set up, rules are strict, and everyone is there trying to make a buck.

The Disney comparison is behind why your per capita sales decrease as attendance rises. There are too many distractions with everyone trying to engage audience members. Crowd and environment noise are extremely high, making communication more difficult. Even the flashiest booths and setups fade into the background as anyone vending will have top of the line graphics in order stay visible. And even when you do engage a customer, because of the sheer number of them, you will never be able to talk with them all, which reduces your effectiveness and limits the time you can spend building a relationship that leads to sales. In Lord of the Rings, Bilbo tells Gandalf, "I feel thin, sort of stretched, like butter scraped over too much bread." There is simply not enough of you to go around—even if you purchase multiple spaces and enlist quality sales help, you will have a glass ceiling based on the tier dynamics.

I'll recap those definitions for you:

Tier 4. Under 1,000 attendees. (Usually 1-2 days in length, sometimes 3.)

Tier 3. 1,000 - 3,000 attendees. (Usually 1-2 days in length, sometimes 3.)

Tier 2. 5,000 - 20,000 attendees. (Usually 2-3 days in length, sometimes 4.)

Tier 1. 40,000 - 100,000 attendees. (Usually 4-5 days in length, sometimes up to 7.)

One is tempted to assume that Tier 1 is the best option. That is not necessarily the case. My preference is actually a mid-sized Tier 2 based on how much additional labor and expense is involved with any show at 25,000 or more.

Remember that you have some static costs such as a booth/table fee, travel costs, food, and the cost of your products (books). You're probably going to eat anyway, even if you stayed at home and binged Netflix. If you bring your food and avoid eating out, you can minimize that cost. I purchased a high-mileage, used hybrid for my convention-mobile, getting me 45mpg to keep the costs low, but with a limitation of how much product I can bring. I will also drive up to 20 minutes and risk a skin rash at terrible/cheap motels—I'm there to work/sell and don't consider my trip a vacation. As a general rule, I make an average profit of about $10 per book sold, which makes the math easy.

I only do Tier 3 shows if they are within a 5-hour drive of me, and Tier 4 if they are within 3. That rule changes if I have a free place to stay such as a relative or friend who will let me couch surf, or if the show brings me in as a guest (which usually means they pay my lodging and table expenses in exchange for teaching a panel, workshop, or being a keynote speaker.) Your booth fee will increase based on the bigger attendance and your other costs will increase too. Some additional costs will also creep in such as parking expenses and additional time spent to set up, pass security checks, etc. That may mean an additional night's stay.

Here are a few general scenarios to see the math in action from shows I've done recently:

Tier 2 show (about 25k attendees) was a 2-hour drive and a local friend covered my lodging, so fuel was negligible in my gas miser. Sold about 200 books in 3 days with a $250 table fee. Paid parking. I grossed about $2,000 after book costs. Was about $30 to park and I ate out one night. That made my total costs about $300, meaning my actual gross was about $1,700 for that weekend.

Tier 1 show (about 40k attendees) was an 800-mile drive making gas about $50 in my hybrid. I sold on the low end because I got placement with poor visibility (I'll talk about that later) and my booth fee was $600 plus lodging of about $250, but no parking fees. I did have about $100 in food costs. With costs of about $1,050, my gross was about $2,500, meaning I made about $1,450. I actually made less money *and* spent nearly 30 hours on the road just driving there and back. Had my booth placement been better, I would have hoped for something closer to $3,500 gross and I could have paid for a cheaper option on my vendor space (which, in hindsight, would have had better visibility.) Had those both happened, I would have saved about $200 and increased hypothetical sales ($3,500-850) I would have grossed about $2,650 and believe it could have been a thousand dollars higher than that if the crowd had been sized as it was pre-COVID. Still, that $2,600 is only about $1,000 more than the Tier 3 show, but with a lot more work and a 600% increase in drive time. Remember, time spent traveling can't be used for much else unless you have a driver, use audio transcription for writing, or are binging audiobooks while driving (my personal preference).

Tier 4 show (about 300 attendees) was on the far side of my travel range, but this was still a daytrip. Attendance was supposed to make it a Tier 3 show, but we hit a perfect storm of COVID concerns, the surrounding area was mired in road construction, etc. Many vendors failed to sell a single item. I did alright at about 30 sales, which is a per cap of 10%. My booth fee was $50. Because the travel was a little further than I generally like, the travel cost was around $20. Estimate $300-700 for a $230 gross on a day's worth of work. A long day, but I made a few new fans at the event, which is also a bonus.

Tier 3A show (about 2,000 attendees) was about a 4-hour drive and I found cheap lodging with a short drive. Lodging and gas combined were about $180, and the convention fee was only $40. I sold 80 books. We can ballpark this at about $600 after expenses for a 2-day con.

Tier 3B show (about 1200 attendees) was a 2-hour drive in the same city as the Tier 2, meaning I was able to also ditch the extra expenses and couch surf. I sold about 60 books with a $125 table fee. $600 versus $125 in expenses gave me around a $500 gross, but it was a 3-day event, requiring a greater time investment.

Another thing to remember is that the lower tier shows tend to let you spend more time with attendees and that typically creates more meaningful relationships. That means that the reader is more likely to become a super fan and/or buy all your books. It is not uncommon at Tier 4 and 3 shows to have a customer buy one of everything (or 5-12 books for most authors ... that stat gets a little scaled back if you have 30 different books on your table). If you have a strong series, though, it is not uncommon to sell the whole series run to a few customers.

Travel time and the length of the show are factors you may want to consider. If I factor in the total time invested in the shows listed above, it reflects my daily income.

Tier 1. 2650 ÷ 5 = $530 (though I really should add another day since 5 x 13-hour days aren't really feasible. That would make it about $440 per day.)

Tier 2. 1700 ÷ 3 = $560 per day.

Tier 3A. 600 ÷ 3 = $200 per day.

Tier 3B. 500 ÷ 2 = $250 per day.

Tier 4. 230 per day.

These are not hard and fast rules, merely examples that fall within the typical norms, which I consider about $200-400 for Tiers 3 and 4, and $300-500 for Tiers 1 and 2. Those are numbers for someone with experience and who knows how to hustle. The rest of this book will teach you what I do to make that my norm. I do believe my numbers can, and will, increase far beyond these as I continue to improve both craft, product, and sales skills.

Initially, my goal was not to make huge profits or replace my day job. I only had a couple of books. None of my series were completed and my table setup wasn't highly appealing. My goal was to break even on my booth/table cost, which was typically $125-250 at most of my events. I was just trying to hit 15-30 books at first, over a 2-or 3-day event. Averaging ten sales per day was pretty great for that mindset. That was a baseline I established, and then I improved and scaled up from there, all the while releasing more books and improving every aspect of my event presence. Now, I hate to sell less than 30 books per day. My point is that you have to start somewhere. Don't expect the above numbers straight out of the gate and understand that these numbers might be much lower than what you are capable of.

Also, remember that you cannot expect to build a budget on doing a large convention every week. Those larger conventions come along with less frequency and getting into them is often difficult at earlier stages in your career. You also must really know the ins and outs of the kinds of shows. That brings us to the next part

Christopher D. Schmitz

… you absolutely *must* know your audience. If I show up at a 50,000-person knitting convention with books, my science fiction isn't likely to do nearly as well as at a Star Trek convention, no matter how good a salesperson I am.

Your audience dictates which kinds of shows you should attend. You can make sales anywhere; we're concerned with maximizing your sale potential. It's *Sell* More *Books*, not *Sell a Few and Be Happy*. We'll drill down on your audience in the coming pages.

Show Tiers Reference

I use this verbiage through the book and decided it would be handy to have a quick reference page to describe them. This does not describe the *type* of show, but it breaks down some of the specifics regarding hard numbers. I understand that there are some squishy bits in the numbers. That is on purpose. You cannot think too rigidly about these classifications as a 4,000-attendee show might feel much like a tier 3 event or it may feel like a tier 2 show, and the factors that give it this feeling are hard to define.

Tier 4
Under 1,500 attendees. (Usually 1-2 days in length, sometimes 3)
Approximate Cost: $50-110
Sales Target: 45 books
Attendance Target: 4%

Tier 3B
2,000 - 5,000 attendees. (Usually 1-2 days in length, sometimes 3)
Approximate Cost: $100-200
Sales Target: 90 books
Attendance Target: 4-5%

Tier 3A
1,000 - 3,000 attendees. (Usually 1-2 days in length, sometimes 3)
Approximate Cost: $75-150
Sales Target: 60 books
Attendance Target: 2-3%

Tier 2

5,000 - 20,000 attendees. (Usually 2-3 days in length, sometimes 4)

Approximate Cost: $75-300

Sales Target: 150 books

Attendance Target: 1-1.5%

Tier 1

40,000 - 100,000 attendees. (Usually 4-5 days in length, sometimes up to 7)

Approximate Cost: $250-600

Sales Target: 300 books

Attendance Target: 0.25-0.5%

Chapter Three: identify your audience

Defining an Audience

Identity is a funny thing. Legacy media often talks in terms of identity politics and it likes to put labels on things. I'm steering clear of all that except to say that a person's perception of themselves is everything to that person. The reason identity politics has become such a hot issue is this: erasing the acknowledgment of a human's self-expression is very much like erasing the person. At least, *that is how the person being erased feels.* I just used a lot of extra words to say that a person's identity is supremely important.

Understanding the supremacy of it pushes us to recognize the impact of knowing who we are selling to. You can't sell every book the same way to every person.

It is a temptation when asked, "Who is your book's audience," to answer "everybody." We all want "all the readers." That answer is a rookie mistake. Identify your best fit; it's okay to call them out when you see them and invite that person to your table to take a look.

Knowing who your readers are is the key to selling well. And *no* ... your book is not for everyone. I understand that we all want as many readers as we can get. But your book is *not* for everybody. No book is. For a book to please everyone, it would have to be so watered down so as not to offend that it would become boring and, therefore, good for nobody. To quote Syndrome from The Incredibles who wanted to give everyone powers, "When everyone's super ... no one will be." Having superpowers sounds pretty good ... but remember that Syndrome was the villain.

I give you permission to zero in on a niche. Go ahead and write your goat-farmers of Neptune romance or a children's encyclopedia of all the kid-devouring monsters that live in suburban closets. A fantasy tale about the lives of socks who must venture into the rotating inferno vortex? I'd read it. An erotic romance between a woman and a fish? Go for it (but remember that Hollywood already did that one ... like multiple times, actually.)

It is easier to find an audience when you drill down into a niche than by attempting to pitch the next great American novel. Forget what your high school English teacher said about what good literature looks like. Just write what appeals to you. Someone else is going to be into that, too.

Let's look at that "someone else." Board games are one of my favorite pastimes, including RPGs (role-playing games). If you're unfamiliar, the most well-known game is Dungeons & Dragons. This exercise is going to feel a little like that because RPGs are, at their heart, an imagination-reality simulator.

One great thing about games like D&D is that you really don't need to know much about the game or its mechanics because the game's operator (GM or DM is the usual lingo,) will handle that. You just tell him or her what you want to do. Whether you can do those things well will be represented by stats on a character sheet.

A character sheet has a bunch of entries on it, including your differing physical and mental stats, special abilities, and most importantly a place to complete a character's back story. Everything in an RPG is designed to make you an important character in the story. In fact, many RPGs ditched that moniker years ago when D&D had earned a bad rap and adopted the name "Storytelling Game." An RPG's character sheet is a tool to help participants play a game of cooperative make-believe.

The sheet we will create helps an author identify who they are selling to; it is a sketch of an archetype of the person that is his or her ideal audience. Give the character a name. Write a bit of history. Insert them into a short story someday—but don't skip this step, even if it feels silly to you.

This idea is not original to me, and many marketers have recommended it for years. I first encountered it at a workshop run by some fellow indie authors some time ago, and I still remember some of the characters we thought up and presented.

While you obviously can't sell books to fictitious people, this exercise helps you think about your audience. It humanizes them and makes you speculate on the types of folks you may encounter while selling books. You can't build the required relationships with ideas, but this prepares you for those future conversations with your target audience.

Your imaginary reader is a caricature of what your buyers will be like—who they are. This exercise will help you by asking a few basic questions:

What are his or her hobbies?
How does he or she spend a typical weekend?
What is his or her economic situation?
What is his or her education level?
Does he or she have kids and what's their marital status?
How old is he or she?
What kind of media does he or she prefer? (By that I mean stories of all formats.)
What is he or she currently binging on a streaming service, and what have they binged more than once?

What book has he or she read multiple times?

You can also sketch them as a complete person by filling in tertiary details. I'll demonstrate at the end.

You can learn a lot from some of these answers. At my convention booth, I often ask people to play a game with me if they look distracted or exhausted. You may remember the game Desert Island, that the crew of the Office played one episode while stuck outside during a fire drill. I tell people that pirates are planning to maroon them on a desert island. But they're fairly considerate, as far as pirates go, and they plan to swing by a bookstore on their way out of port and will let a person take three books to the island with them. What are your three books?

That question can help you drill down on an audience and build some bridges to books *you like* or allow you to make connections to books you have for sale. It's another tool that can help. And if you don't know any of their book picks, ask them. You can try to fake it—that sometimes works, too—or just change the subject.

Back to your character sketch. One of the additional benefits of this is that it allows you to ask an additional question:

What kind of events would he or she attend in their spare time—or, even better, what events would he or she prioritize?

Some people wait all year for Comic-Con. Brides-to-be will take vacation days to attend a regional wedding expo. Paranormal fans will buy early tickets to see a ghost hunter speak at your local historical society's haunted cemetery event.

The point is that if you know your audience, you'll have an easier time finding events where your ideal buyers will be and what excites them. You'll know what kinds of things make them tick well enough to get books into their hands and which of your titles will most satisfy their souls.

I was at a workshop in a library at the invitation of a few authors I knew, and we discussed marketing. A man I met that night asked my advice on where he could go to sell his books. He couldn't think of anywhere because of what his upcoming book was about; it was a nonfiction title and sort of a wisdom book with personal insights, almost a biography, almost philosophy. This writer had been a columnist for a major sporting magazine (back when people used to buy and read those) called In-Fisherman. You may have leafed through it in your dentist's office. For more than a decade he wrote a monthly page worth of content featuring his thoughts, anecdotes, and insights related to fishing and the real world.

Sitting in a room full of genre fiction authors, he couldn't see a way to market to an audience because of comparison. He wasn't thinking about *his* audience; he could only see ours. That same thing happens when we walk into a bookstore and see the latest flash-in-the-pan YA Urban Fantasy knockoff or some other rehashed plot with a new cover based on the upcoming movie. Don't worry about someone else—go get *your* audience.

I explained that his market was maybe the easiest to find. He had a built-in base. "Nonfiction is easier to sell because it answers specific questions or hits on specific, tangible interests. Your background also makes you an expert. You should immediately find every Spring Sports and Boating show you can find, even lawn and garden shows. Get a banner that advertises you as a long-time author at that magazine and set up a table right next to the bass boats. Then you've got many options at shows through the year, gun shows, camping expos, wherever there is a crossover audience. But make two books. Nostalgia sells, so if you've got the rights or if you can get them, compile a collection of all your old articles. Nothing sells a book like having two books."

I have provided a sample sketch of a person I envision as a prime candidate for my Dekker's Dozen series, which gets favorable comparison to the Firefly/Serenity TV show/film. The instant connection is there based on an article of clothing often worn by fans of the show … there may be crossover appeal after learning about other interests that would make them interested in my fantasy as well.

…I can literally hear the conversations with her in my head and I'm pretty certain I've met this particular person at four or five past events.

(The following sheets are available as printable documents and can be found at www.authorchristopherdschmitz.com/authorservices.)

Character Sheet

Overview: Ava has a toddler and husband in tow and dressed in an old Metallica concert T. She is wearing a "Jayne hat," from Firefly and the two teenagers she shares with husband are wandering near.

She appears middle aged, wears glasses, and her husband is carrying a bag with fresh purchases, so you know they are buying.

Name: Ava
Age: 44
Family Details: Ava is divorced but remarried with blended family. She and Joe have 3 kids, one is both theirs

Job: Gas Station Mgr.

Economics: 84k comb. lower middle class?

Interests: Star Trek, MCU films, live concerts, camping

Life Goals: no particular goals or 5 yr plan. Says she plans to run for school board, but never will

Event: Tier 3B comiccon

Location: lives in nearby rural town. Owns a cramped home w/ Joe

Education: Completed one year towards her A.A. before drpping out

Favorite Books: LOTR
Harry Potter
Dune

Bingeable Media: Shannarra Chronicles, ST:DS9

Media Preferences: Paperbacks only occasional audiobook

Marketing Channels: Facebook, Snap, Pinterest junky

Other: Ava was always a trekkie and a SF fan because it spoke to her inner nerd and socially rebellious nature.

She was a huge Buffy the Vampire fan in the 1990s and identified most with Willow, rather than Buffy.

Ava and Joe used to play a D&D game every week. They haven't played in 2 yrs, but in their mind it is still going, as if they played last week.

Blank Character Sheet

Overview:

Name:
Age:
Family Details:

Interests:

Life Goals:

Job:

Economics:

Event:

Location:

Education:

Favorite Books:

Bingeable Media:

Media Preferences:

Marketing Channels:

Other:

Chapter Four: Before You Attend a Show

The Big Why

Not to sound like a prima donna actor, but ask yourself, "What's my motivation?"

I promise that we will talk about practical, tangible things pretty much from here on out, but it is imperative that you understand your motivations as a seller first. If you don't understand the system and yourself (including your goals and what drives you to do this), then you may be doomed to fail. Even if you succeed wildly, but without understanding, you'll hit a glass ceiling or struggle to scale this side of the business and that frustration will lead to burnout.

Frustration is real and I really hate to see folks burn out. Take measures to prevent the pitfalls that this industry (and sales in general) can present.

Instead of "motivation," ask yourself the question, "Why do I want to do live sales?" Let's break down some common answers. I will also point out the trappings of each motivation along the way.

It's a great way to cut through the noise and get more eyes on my book.

This can be true, and it is easy to feel the difference. If you've ever launched a book online, you've probably checked in at your digital sales board only to find it sitting there … doing nothing. It's hard to pierce through the digital noise and distractions of the internet—heck, you can't even get in touch with folks by posting to your own social media anymore without paying a bunch of ad dollars.

While there are billions of people online, they are all competing for the same visibility and that makes for the chaotic, cut-throat world of online marketing. Amateurs with no budget stand little chance against professionals with significant ad-spend at their disposal.

This motivation is fine. And direct sales is a great way to get a piece of the pie, a small and manageable slice. The reason for this is that your audience is focused based on who the attendees are, rather than on every human with an internet connection. (You did the character sheet exercise from the last chapter, right? Right?) Especially at the smaller shows, you will find the greatest success because your niche audience is present, defined, and likely primed to make purchases with the least amount of competition.

Caution: this all sounds well and good but remember that you will have a glass ceiling. You may also find that it is difficult to get exposure outside your particular niche. While your cozy mystery series about a quilt-making grandmother who is also an amateur sleuth will do well at quilting shows and craft fairs, you will also want folks who are into crime and detective thrillers to be exposed to your books, so be sure to look for crossover niches.

Just like Amazon has "also-boughts," you want to find a way to cross-pollinate with other audiences as well so you won't limit yourself in the long-term. Think about Harry Potter. It's a perfect fit in urban fantasy and coming of age themed events. But do you know who else loves Harry Potter? *Everyone*. Niche your audience but try not to impose too many limits and be looking for other areas to branch out into. To be honest, the same lighting that struck for J. K. Rowling won't likely hit you, but the more you branch out with additional books that are different by only a matter of degrees, the more manageable avenues and sales channels you will discover.

I need more exposure for my book/want to find more followers.

For the sake of your long-term success, authors want to find and engage with an audience. That means building a following, people who are going to be future warm doors to your sales channels and who have a genuine interest in what you are doing. In the business, we call this a *platform*. Building an author platform is a critical part of your role.

There are many avenues to building up your platform, and I've found that my readers who are the most engaged with my social media and newsletter are folks who I have personally met and conversed with at events. (There's that relationship thing again.) To have a platform, you've got to get people. You can get them online by things like group promos, paid services, and newsletter swaps, but just like trying to sell books online, you have to deal with the noise of the internet; you have to find a way to push through. Onboarding people onto your platform is a little easier than selling a product, but it's still got the same kinds of difficulties as the above motivation. I should be clear here, getting sign-ups sometimes goes hand in hand with making sales, but it is a distinctly different animal, and there are whole books out there that address it.

Caution: There is a temptation to avoid here that which I've already discussed: make sure not to substitute this motivation for another. When a show doesn't go as planned, you could throw up your hands and say, "At least I got a dozen new subscribers to my newsletter/social media."

But you can't pay the light bill with Facebook likes.

If you have a bad show or two, it is understandable that you will want to take away *something* to validate why you are doing live shows that turn out to be financial losses. But if you have multiple, consecutive shows that performed poorly, or the majority of your events have to be validated with the "exposure" excuse, that is indicative of a problem that you need to address and you should ask others for honest advice (be sure to give explicit permission for them to give brutal feedback. Tense yourself and prepare for some harsh realities, probably regarding covers or your sales pitch, or other fundamentals.) Accept honest criticism and find one or two things you can change now and then work on the rest as you move forward.

I want to meet potential industry contacts.

I have met a lot of folks who are non-author literary professionals at live events of all sizes. These include librarians, bookstore owners, book buyers (those who make bulk purchases for businesses including distributors,) literary agents, television and media personalities, and event promoters.

All of these contacts are great to have and can further your career. I mentioned previously that I've done television, blog, radio, and podcast interviews. Most of those have come about from meeting people at large events and building a connection. It's led to me being placed on bookstore shelves, getting some organic advertising, and making even more contacts with the kinds of folks that are critical to professional success.

Caution: just because some folks have success with this, it doesn't mean you will have it. There is a certain amount of gambling with any business venture, and you need to be treating this like a business to have any *actual* success.

A secondary caution should be issued as well, just because you meet someone claiming to be a professional, that doesn't make it true. People, given a small amount of anonymity, can say whatever they like about themselves and probably two-thirds of the people I've met have told outright lies about the actual degree of their clout. Anonymity is great in one aspect—you can confidently present yourself as being the most amazing author that audiences have never heard of ... but soon will—and that can help you craft your live events and lead to more sales and success. However, on the other edge of that knife, folks will claim to be big shot literary agents, publishing agents, or the like and want to try to slice off a wedge of your cheddar. You will want to verify credentials. Never surrender the cheddar.

I mentioned having folks make big claims that have turned out to be grossly exaggerated or downright false. One guy told me he was close friends with E.L. James who might be interested in finding a new ghostwriter... I only heard back from James when her lawyer sued me in early 2022 (which is a funny story about her trademark lawyers trying to bully me about using the line "50 Shades of Worf." I won, BTW ... well, I got them to drop the case at least, which was a shame since a full-blown lawsuit would've given me a ton of publicity.) I've seen fake publishers and literary agents hoodwinking many authors into bad deals meant to stuff the pockets of charlatans; there's no shortage of grifters and there are reasons my articles exposing fraud are the most read pieces on my blog.

All of this is to say: know what sharks in suits look like and where to find details on industry norms. Many sites compile known fake publishers and agents. We authors stick together. Find yourself an author mentor who can help keep you from getting bit.

I want to network with other authors.

This is a great idea. There is a shared sense of camaraderie in mutual suffering. I haven't often felt like conventions are a form of pain, but they do require work, and that can translate to some degree of pain. I've made a lot of author and artist friends while tabling at the same shows. We have shared meals, travel expenses, and even split rooms and fees to attend past events, reducing the cost of buy-in for larger shows.

One of the most fun aspects of this is engaging in after parties. Many conventions or shows will take place in hotel convention centers. This is especially true of niche-focused tier 4 and 3 events. My wife doesn't particularly share in the majority of my fandoms (she didn't realize she was marrying a sci-fi and fantasy junky), but she does enjoy attending the surreal experience that can be a convention room party. Some events will also host professional networking-specific events for the vendors, and one artist-heavy show I do actually provides a supper and a green room experience for those lucky enough to pass jury and table there.

In addition to looking for these connections at sales events, you should also keep an eye out for local and regional author conferences and workshops that have an educational component. They will often feature industry contacts and become informational settings rather than sales opportunities; most of the ones that I've been to have had only very small, if any, vendor spaces. These have proven to be great connection points for me and they often have genre-based info tracks you can participate in which will help you locate like-minded people.

Caution: not everyone wants to be your friend. I had a particularly good show where I had brought a friend who was adept at sales. We set a high goal for the three-day show and had practically run out of items to sell halfway through. The artist on the opposite side of the aisle stared daggers at us the whole time. She didn't attempt to engage a single patron, but she did entertain an obvious desire to murder us. Once envy set in, her attitude kept her from having any success or any fun.

Jealousy can be a very real thing among booth neighbors, and this is one reason I prefer to not be placed directly adjacent to other authors. I know my presence is solid, and I don't want other authors to be discouraged or suffer a seeming lack of sales by any attempted comparison.

The second caution I would throw up is to be careful not to overindulge in a room party. Even if you are the host, there is an inherent risk in reducing boundaries too far and letting in unsavory elements. Vetting is not usually done well and security is usually lax at after parties. I remember waiting for hours to catch an Uber back to my hotel (my room was a cheaper option a mile down the road and my table help had driven that day.) I was delayed as I had to sit up until three in the morning with another vendor that I only barely knew to prevent him from driving home drunk. It was a superhero convention, and it was time to put on my own cape and keep someone from making a bad decision. That happens in life, not just at hotel parties… but be sure *not to be that guy*. Know your limits, keep tight boundaries, and bring your own chaperone or designated driver if you plan to cut loose a little. But remember that nothing will ruin your convention experience or reputation faster than getting stupid at an after party.

I just want people to read and enjoy my book.

This sounds like a pure and altruistic approach. Surely there can't be any pitfalls to being motivated by the pure love of reading? You'd be wrong, but let's talk about the motivation first.

It's a great motivation. The heart of a storyteller beats strong in you and you want to spin worlds into motion by the power of your words, much like Tolkien's Ilúvatar did in the Ainulindalë Legendarium. You are driven to create, and I think that is amazing: a glimmer of divinity represented in all humankind by our drive to make things as a reflection of our God-given Imago Dei.

The fact that people will read your stories is what gives them purpose. You aren't just writing for your own amusement. You're not a writer—you're an *author*. Your books have their greatest meaning when they are read; your characters don't truly live except when they find root in the soil of someone else's mind.

This motivation carries much weight and is the motivation of a pure artist. Money and even acknowledgment that you were the author are secondary to the story itself. Fame and payment are nice, but because they don't drive you, it doesn't wreck your world if those things never come.

Caution: the warning here is in getting too wrapped up in what others think of your book. You have to be willing to be disappointed to be an author, or any kind of artist. I sold a person a full series of my explicitly faith-based high fantasy series which reads like Game of Thrones meets C. S. Lewis. The woman was very excited. I saw this same person at a different show months later and was selling to her when she stopped me to tell me about a book she'd bought from some guy recently, "It was great. I loved it … until it started bringing God into it." She'd forgotten me but remembered the book.

After letting her trash my series for a bit, I told her I remembered her, but didn't bring up how I had told her explicitly that this was a dark fantasy written from a Christian perspective including a war between angels and demons, so God would be intrinsic to the content. But I write tons of secular stuff, too. I gave her my contact info and told her that if she didn't like my Esfah series, she could reach out to me, and I'd buy the books back from her. Turns out they were a good fit.

The danger here is in relying too much on wanting a good report back. I've given away books before, and of all those I've given for free, I can't say I've ever had one produce a review I could trace or a follow up sale. When you give something away, the recipient psychologically ascribes it a zero-dollar value and so it loses importance. The books you buy and hand out probably go unread. I used to run a music venue for teenagers, and we'd pay regionally popular bands to come and play. Attendance was falling dramatically until I realized this principle; we began charging $2-5 at the door. Teens thought it was valuable now, but it remained affordable and so attendance shot up ... and on the book note, hearing back from fans is pretty rare. However, folks who *hate* you are more than willing to share that fact. If the love of a story is your only motivation, it's a recipe for discouragement.

To tell the truth, I just want to make some money!

This is honest. And it is also fine motivation; I'd argue it might be the most important one! Too many people have a negative stigma about wanting to earn, thinking it degrades their art or is a selfish motivation. At some point, you've got to pay the bills, and you can't give the electric company free copies of your latest ebook in trade, so get over any moral hang-ups you have about wanting to make money. If it bothers you to trade currency for a valuable thing you produce, then I will gladly take the difference—I'll even put it to good use.

More seriously, anybody who completely overlooks the monetary aspect of this business cheapens their intrinsic value and, as mentioned before, psychologically conditions people to *not read* their book. This is a business, after all, and you must treat it as such. That may feel dirty for some people who really hate charging for any form of art. Unless you're privately wealthy and want to treat this author thing as if it's a charity you hope to bless the world with, demand your worth (and yes, I've seen that "bless the world" book. A while back, an American wrote a very sad little memoir about abuse and struggling with gender identity and sexual preference issues but then found Jesus and became wealthy selling furniture or something [I only skimmed it.] The person then printed hundreds of thousands of copies and mass-mailed them to huge swaths of people. On a whim I looked it up on Amazon to check reviews. They're about as bad as expected when you release a sub-par product to a hostile audience you have zero credibility with while also deeply insulting a large segment of the population. [Side note, as an actual licensed minister—and not the kind of license bought on the internet, Jesus is much more about sharing faith through relationships than guerrilla-style ambush evangelism.]

If you don't look at your book with a business eye, you're likely to release a garbage product. It sounds harsh, but it is true. If you won't treat your book seriously by investing in it with quality cover art and layouts, paying an editor to hurt your feelings, and spending hundreds of maddening hours in rewrites, then your resulting book will be sub-par. If you don't anticipate making money on it, you'll fall into a mindset of, "Meh, it's good enough." And trust me, I've seen that book, and no, it's not. I know, because in my early days, I did exactly that. I maybe did 90% of what was necessary—but 90% investment only earns you about 5% of what you should. Anybody who is serious in the indiesphere is hustling at 100% and so you've got to put in 95% just to earn 25%. I know, these numbers don't make sense, but you've got to go the extra mile—there are some people out there who are killing it. They aren't your competition, per se, but they are your comparison.

Caution: money is a noble and necessary purpose, but it cannot be everything. Do not be too greedy. If closing the sale is your only goal, despite the needs and preferences of the person you are selling to, it will come back to bite you, usually in the form of negative publicity or bad reviews.

When you are talking to someone and trying to close a sale, you need to get them excited about the book and connect it to his or her passions. Sometimes, that person just doesn't have any relevant interests. It is fine to let them walk away and invite them back if they ever gain an appreciation for something like your fandom. _It's okay not to sell to everyone._

Thinking only from that "hafta close every sale and make a buck" mindset is going to encourage high-pressure sales tactics, guilt tripping people, or outright lying to cash in. I mentioned reputation previously. You may find yourself not invited back to an event, or on the rightful end of some negative reviews if you fall too deeply into this pit.

A middle ground exists where you can present your book to your best audience, and they will gladly pay for your book—and even come back to buy again. That perfect scenario happens when you keep your customers' satisfaction paramount—and happy customers gladly reward you with coin of the realm.

Selling in person seems an easier way to make sales than online.

I mentioned earlier that some folks find great difficulty in piercing through the digital noise. This is a specific trouble I have, although I naturally engage people in the real world with relative ease. But you are not me; your skill with people could be worlds better or you could be terrified of even leaving your house if it means interacting with other humans.

Jerry Seinfeld jokes about a survey of peoples' worst fears: death being ranked below public speaking, which means most people would rather be in the coffin than giving the eulogy. I *understand* that sentiment, although I have never had a problem with getting up in front of a group and speaking, not even in school. Some of us are just built differently. My wife is an introvert and seldom does shows with me—when we meet new people, I have to start the conversations. I understand that some folks have as equal a difficulty at selling live as others do via virtual techniques.

If you struggle to get the sales you need with digital systems such as Amazon, Kobo, and other online booksellers, this is certainly a great alternative. The profit margin is also much higher. One of the reasons that many authors go the indie publishing route is that the per-sale royalties are so much better. Before throwing in hard on the indie model, I had received a few absurdly small royalty checks in the mail, causing me to check my calculations on what I was earning per book. By way of comparison, that book is now an indie title and 99 cents on Amazon; at the lowest royalty rate I will still earn slightly more per sale than when a traditional publisher was selling it at full price—the difference is that I am out there motivated to sell it, whereas the publisher had a laisez faire attitude toward promoting it. By that, I mean they did not.

In the same way, you can make a lot more money with fewer sales by selling paperbacks and being able to control all the factors. I'll demonstrate more on that later, but the novel above was a series starter in my *Wolves of the Tesseract* urban fantasy series. Publishers give a discount on author copies, but as some smaller companies do, they inflate the price slightly beyond industry norms, meaning my paperback was 18.99 when it should have been 14.99 and my author copies, based on the discount, cost me 14.25 to buy (unless I bought in huge quantities). I get twice the profit and a much easier sale at the 14.99 consumer price point. (Remember to check out the bonus supplement on pricing as well.)

An additional benefit of live/paperback sales versus online sales is on the returns side. I write about both returns and pricing structures in the Pricing Hacks bonus chapter, but there has been a lot of talk in the Indie community about the unfair return model enforced by Amazon (it's mandated by the KU Terms Of Service.) It allows unscrupulous readers to buy an ebook, read it fully, and then return it for a full refund; some prominent authors are seeing massive returns and for some, it's been enough to make some authors who are used to big paydays *actually owe Amazon money instead of earning royalties* because all returns have to be repaid (actually the author also must pay a distribution fee, too). In all my years selling live, I've had only one return and that was because a buyer was afraid they weren't going to make rent otherwise. Both regular and creative forms of book piracy are a much lesser issue for copies sold at live events.

Because indies have total control over their pricing structure as well as all other aspects of their business, you can tweak the elements to ensure you maximize your ability to sell. You have the power to perfectly balance your book's salability against profit, and that's a great place to be in as a business owner.

Caution: don't put all your eggs in one basket.

Financial experts agree that the best path to wealth is with multiple sources of revenue. For your investments to perform well, your broker will insist that you diversify your holdings. When one channel performs poorly, the others may do better, and a wise investment firm will continue to tweak and modify your accounts until your portfolio is producing returns as well as it can on all fronts.

Running a business is the same. And this is a business. (I'm going to sound like a broken record on this point and all through the book.) I've used the analogy of a stool with your live events being one of the legs. The more legs you have, the less likely it is to tip over. Ideally, you can have strong success on Amazon and digital outlets, but you can also do well with sales from your own personal website. (I actually do well with that since I control that digital space.) It's nice to also make sales to libraries (yes, you should be paid for those copies, even though the readers won't have to), and to also be on bookstore shelves. Each of those is a different leg—and live events tend to be my bread and butter since it's proved the easiest way for me—but I'm still learning and working to strengthen those other legs.

Whatever legs you need to establish, or whatever channels you need to fix, *do it*. I'm sure that for many of you, that is the reason you purchased this book, to add an additional leg to your current model.

Hopefully you've read the above list and thought, "I have all of those motivations." That is the point. You need to put some stock in all of them, but also not rely on any one of them too heavily.

Understanding your motivations means you're ready to get ready. I know how stupid that sounds, but we're going with it, anyway. Once you have a handle on the *why* and have set some *expectations*, you can look at the practical steps to doing events.

We looked at your audience and tried to figure out where your best market will be. Hopefully you came up with a list of appealing events while crafting some of those character sheets.

Wherever those hypothetical readers are pointing you is a good place to begin scheduling events.

I'm about to give you a checklist of things you may want to consider. We'll talk about each of them a little more through the rest of the book, which gets ever more pragmatic from here on out. Each of these requires different kinds of skills and assets to pull off well; just start somewhere and progressively improve. Remain open to critical feedback and look at frustrations as opportunities to improve and hone your presentation … it's all editing and rewriting, but in real life. Just like editing and rewriting, *don't take every piece of advice, either*. Keep your voice, and understand that in our culture, everyone feels like they need to be constantly acting as experts. One person told me they hated one of my covers (usually cause for alarm) and insisted that it needed changing. That cover was halfway through a 7-book series and yes, it wasn't traditional for the genre, but it was consistently the first book from the series that people picked up. It was out of the norm, but it was effective.

What we haven't yet discussed is the most imperative asset. *Time*. We'll do that here, briefly, and assume from here on out that each of the required things has its own time commitment that you will want to consider.

Everything from brushing your teeth, to brewing coffee, to pooping takes time. It's easy to forget and we build it into our estimates. But what about when you don't know how long something takes? Most of us tend to make assumptions. If you're like me, those assumptions are often wrong. You will want to pre-plan as much of your live events as possible until you are comfortable with them.

Pre-plan many aspects of them even *after* you are comfortable.

Most large events have rigid timelines that you have to respect as a potential vendor. If you have a free weekend ten days from now, it's the wrong time to try booking the event. You might be able to pick up a Tier 4 show on a whim, but organizers generally need more notice than days or weeks—it's usually months.

Remember, also, that it takes time to get additional books printed and shipped to you if they're not already on hand. Hotels and B&Bs often book up further out than that, and if you need to schedule time off from work, you'll want better planning.

As an example, the San Diego Comic Convention (one of the three biggest comic-cons in the USA) opens its application period about ten months before the event and it fills up fast. The same goes for most of the Tier 1 shows that I do. Keep a calendar and track what shows you've applied to (not every show is guaranteed and they have their own submission guidelines to watch). I also track which ones I've paid for, been wait-listed for, and my sales goals and past actual results so I can decide if it's a show I should continue doing. (It's how I got the data I share later in this book).

The more you track, the better you'll be. Understand that the more prepared you are, the better your results will be, as well. Start small and scale up. Tier 4 shows are a great place to cut your teeth. Then scale up into Tier 3 and 2. I suggest waiting until you are very comfortable and can set reasonable sales and expense expectations before jumping into a tier 1 event.

If I were setting a calendar for a beginning author, I would tell them to book one Tier 2 show and expect they will lose a little money doing it. That show would be 6-8 months away and I would book a couple of Tier 3 shows and a couple of Tier 4 shows spread between now and the Tier 2 date.

Now, on to the checklist, which we'll break down in future chapters.

Checklist

Booking:

Money and Time enough to pay table fees and apply

Plan to cover your lodging (hotel, B&B, box under an overpass, etc.)

Vehicle to get you to the show and enough space to carry books & signage

Goals made, and expectations set

Food and drink if you plan to bring your own

Proper sales tax registration (varies from location to location)

Tech:

Credit Card Reader/point of sale

Emergency power supply

Apps installed on smartphone in case of problems with credit card reader

Source of Wi-Fi (such as hot spot capability)

Alternative payment options

Sales tax setup in point of sale

Booth:

Know your table/booth placement

Tables/chairs (know if they are provided or if you must supply)

Newsletter sign-up device (tech or pen & paper)

Enough change to handle cash

Table Covers

Signage

Book stands/display items

Bookmarks, flyers, or other promotional materials

Collapsible cart to carry supplies and products

Emergency supply kit

Chapter Five: Finding Your Events

Earlier, we did an exercise to identify a target audience. Before moving on, I want to talk some about the types of events that you might consider and look at how your target affects these events.

When I identified the best source of where *my* audience was I came into comic book conventions. There are many types of comic-cons, all sub-divided by nuance, but I'll lump them together as a type of convention even though I assume at the outset that I'll sell more horror and dark fantasy at horror-themed cons than at anime cons. And I'll sell high numbers of my comic-con murder mystery at pop culture (unthemed or multi-themed) comic conventions.

Summed up, my readers are generally the biggest nerds in the room at any given moment. I have also branched out and now I also sell at renaissance festivals and board game conventions. I know that's where I'll find the kinds of people who like my books, so that's where I go.

But first, let's talk about live events that *aren't* those huge events, but where we can find similarity and overlap.

Bookstore Signings. This is what most people think about when doing live events. You can thank Hollywood for that. If you have a picture in your head about what that looks like but realize that the image is drawn from television or movies, then your idea is likely wrong. It looks more like being a greeter at a box store. At least it looks that way if you're anything ranked lower than the top 250 on Amazon (yes—I mean in *the whole store.*)

The store will probably give you a small table with some books on it and, if you're lucky, they may have done some small promotion for you or placed a sign for you. Mostly, you'll be greeting people cold and asking if you can tell them about your book while giving directions to the restrooms.

There is value in doing these events, but not as much as you'd think. The audience isn't focused by genre like it is at a themed show; if they expect three hundred store visitors through the doors while you're there, maybe a quarter of them are a relevant audience and that means increased rejections while you talk to folks. And since almost none of them came in to see *you*, don't expect a lot of sales—but you should be able to create enough value in selling autographed copies that you should make *some* sales.

These signings aren't difficult to secure. You usually just need to know who to ask, and workers are typically helpful in pointing managers out to you. Smaller stores will often have you consign books so that the store keeps a percentage. Larger stores will often purchase them through distribution (and won't buy them from Amazon so you'll need to be setup in Ingram or another distributor) and they will want to buy them at the wholesale rate (a 50-55% discount off MSRP) and will want to be able to return overstock.

Warning: make sure you know how many they are planning to order and have an honest and explicit estimate of how many you think you will sell while in the store. I told a manager at a large store, we'll protect identities and call it Narnes and Bobles, and they placed me somewhere even less visible than the bathrooms and ordered 250% of the quantity that I told them I could sell with good placement. I've had great events in the past at other Narnes and Bobles stores, but this one sent all the books back to the distributor the very next day meaning. I lost hundreds of dollars due to returns after spending a day frustrated in the secret catacombs of an urban bookstore. The more straightforward you can be with a store, the better off you'll be. Remember that this is a business for them, too, and honest talk is good for bottom lines.

A brief how-to: because a lot of authors wonder about how to get into a bookstore signing, I'll offer a quick primer.

1. Make sure your book is quality and meets industry standards (buyers can't tell it's an indie title by looking at it, book is professionally edited, etc.)

2. Your book must not have an Amazon owned ISBN (that would alienate +90% of the stores and be viewed as a slap in the face to most owners if you gave them a stack of competitor's books and asked the store to sell them.)

3. Your book must be returnable in their distribution network and have an agreeable wholesale discount. Stores buy a product at a discount so they can sell for a profit. Narnes and Bobles can't buy your $15 book for $15 and then resell it for $15 and continue to exist. 10% isn't enough, either. Most stores' margins are super thin even at 40-55% which is the expected margin range. It's 55% for bigger chains and sometimes larger if they are buying in massive quantities (which would necessitate a bulk printer who does not use the Print on Demand production style most indies lean on.) I set most of my books to 50% in broad distribution in the USA and a lower rate of 40% for overseas; I only accept returns in the USA. You cannot set either the discount or

returnability of your books in Amazon/KDP's system; neither can you change the wholesale rate to anything past 40%. You must use a different company for this; the option used by most indies is Ingramspark.

4. Alternatively, some stores, especially smaller/mom and pop stores, will prefer a consignment arrangement. They'll sell your book but keep a certain percentage. Each store will have their own rules. You'll need to track those details, quantity, and locations on your own.

5. You need to simply ask. Have an elevator pitch prepared to sell *yourself*. You want the stores' gatekeepers to think your presence in the store will be a net gain for their company. A signing should be a win-win choice for both of you.

6. If this event goes well, you may ask them to carry a few copies on their shelves. Often this will be on a consignment basis, and even smaller stores will often be willing to do a consignment without a prior appearance, especially if there is strong local interest.

Library Events. I have done a few of these. One thing has remained consistent about them; they are not well attended. However, libraries often have budgets and I've been paid to do events with them, although they've led to few sales. Even meet and greet style events have been fairly poor but, depending on how much social influence and clout you have locally, this is subject to change. Library patrons are used to *not* making purchases, and sales made will more likely come from the library's book buyer than anywhere else. Luckily, if you have a decent back catalog, you may sell it in its entirety.

While I am often paid directly for an appearance, that is not always the case. And I've already mentioned that sales are not particularly high. However, I think libraries play a critical role in building up and investing into the readers of tomorrow, and we can't measure that kind of karma in dollars.

If you are hoping to make a lot of money breaking into the library market, that will be a tough nut to crack and events with them will be more localized to a particular community or, if you're lucky, to a library network. These can, however, lead to other opportunities, speaking engagements, and will certainly open doors for you that might be otherwise closed.

Book Clubs. These are another kind of meet and greet event, much like library appearances. They are … well … weird. I traveled a long way to do an event with one and books were never even mentioned. I felt like I was living out a meme. A lot of book clubs have little to do with reading, I learned. Others, however, are phenomenal. I did one that was sci-fi specific after making a friend at a con. He bought a few and had the rest of his crew pick up copies online or via direct purchase on my website. The club broadcast their conversation about the book on their YouTube channel. Watching them discuss the book and characters was forty-five minutes of pure joy as I got to watch readers talk about themes and topics as they developed through the books. It was also fun to see the event promoter smirk and mention, "I think I know where he was going with (some of the tropes), since I happen to have had several chats with him and know his background."

These events may bring you a few sales, but they will probably bring more joy than dollars. I don't know the exchange rate on joy to cash, but it works out in favor of doing these when they present themselves, just have clear expectations beforehand. Some libraries will host or sponsor these events, and they might develop out of making contacts at libraries.

Panels/Presentations at Arts Councils. Like libraries, these are often paid appearances. I love doing them for the same reason that I am writing this book: I enjoy helping unravel the publishing mystery for others who wonder about how to best present their art to the world.

This can also turn into more appearances, but not all of them are likely to be paid, and pay is unlikely to ever be high. The "starving artist" concept is alive and well. For instance, I am the top ranked performer in my region on Gigsalad, which is an online booking service for performers. I play the bagpipes, an instrument that is among the hardest to play and is an extremely rare talent; a set of pipes that can even hold tune is almost a thousand dollars at a minimum and I travel an average 4-8 hours roundtrip to play gigs. Even on St. Patrick's Day, I have people trying to lowball me into cut rates and driving a full day or do shows necessitating a hotel (out of my own pocket) while wanting me to employ a rare service on an expensive piece of equipment which I would provide on my busiest day of the year and do so for a net loss of a few hundred dollars. There isn't any money in art.

Except for when there is. Some years I've made over $3,000 on St. Patrick's Day alone between tips and booking fees.

Feel free to say no when relevant and know your worth. This last year, I drove a one-hour round trip and played my pipes for an elementary school at my own expense. The children loved it. It made my heart happy to see six-year-olds dancing in a cafeteria at the sheer love of sound. I turned down multiple paying gigs because they wouldn't pay my required mileage expense with fuel at an all-time high. Sometimes joy is a better dollar, and that's a lesson you have to learn your own way—plus I get skeptical when the person with the pocketbook implies you might not be worth your value. (While I typically make a couple thousand every year on Mar 17 ... one year one bar decided they would only pay half because their attendance was low, and another stiffed me altogether. I negotiate gig contracts separately. Sometimes I throw in a cheap show as filler, but then one booker from a filler show told all the other bars they could get me cheaper, and those that *did* pay refused to honor the original agreements. So maybe I'm gun shy since then, but I refuse to take it on faith that someone values talent if they try to devalue your art during negotiations regarding payment. The desperate bar owners who needed a piper did not get one. Stick to your guns and make that an ideal. Tip your Uber driver and Door Dash driver … there's a reason nobody is picking up your gig. Add a tip and demonstrate that you value someone else's time.).

That said, it is smart to have an idea of your worth before having a conversation about payment for appearances. And if you have no idea what you should charge for your idea, feel free to fake it until you have an idea. I generally charge $200-300 depending on what the event is, plus my travel costs. I will often waive this fee if I really like the idea behind it or really want to make it happen. (Like I said, I threw away paying gigs to play for children, so everything is on the table here.) Many arts councils or groups will have the option of securing grants to pay you, so don't discount yourself unless you have to. This is my same advice for negotiating a payment to be a keynote speaker or panelist at an event.

Small gatherings. This is super vague, I know. But depending on your genre, this could be very lucrative. As a former pastor, I know how much traveling speakers make for small gatherings such as church services and special meetings. Not only is there money available to hire someone who is speaking or providing special music or a talent, but those in attendance will also, very likely, purchase items from a table at the end of the event.

Obviously, you need to know your audience here, but religious folks have a huge edge on this kind of event because of how their audience has been conditioned with a lifetime of expectations. I played as part of a music group for a youth group and had a few books at a table in the back. I sold most of them and had folks order a few titles I had sold out. I believe the band also got a small stipend, too.

If your book(s) are about religious content and you are getting a speaker's fee as well, you are on a good path to both making money and getting your message out to an eager audience. I have a number of faith-based books that I've written, and although I don't pursue this as my primary model, I have worked with and mentored other authors who write only religious books. This is a great avenue with a built-in system to get out the word about your book and get paid to do what you love: share your message and content.

While religious writers and groups have the market cornered, it is not only faith-based writers, however. Nonfiction, in general, can find recurring markets if they have credentials or some sort of expertise in their content. That might include scholarly and research writing, among other topics. Political and social commentaries might also do well here as there are groups abroad that one could query about coming to share your book and expertise on specific subject matter.

Craft shows. These are a type of consumer fair. Much like a swap meet or a "flea market," there is a primary focus on independent vendors who are generally the creators of their merchandise.

There are many kinds of Maker events where you are required to be the creator of your content. This would include things like crafting shows and art shows, although some of them will allow vendors of all types, including folks selling Mary Kay, Amway, Tupperware, and other multi-level marketing schemes. "If you want to get my books free, you need to buy ten of each title and then you get three friends underneath you, see. They start selling the books too, and then I curl my mustache betwixt my fingers and laugh my way to the bank."

Craft shows can do very well, especially as you get nearer the holidays when folks are buying gifts. Around Christmastime, you don't need to be anywhere close to your target audience niche because people aren't necessarily buying for themselves and, as I tell many buyers, "There's nothing quite so special as a personalized and autographed book. I can make this out to whomever you would like."

Perhaps the best part about these events is that they are a lot like swap meets. People come expecting to spend money. They may have some entertainment or workshops and speakers, but everyone passing through the doors plans to either spend cash or browse goods to consider purchasing. That mindset makes it easier to ask for the sale.

Trade shows. Like craft shows and consumer fairs, the audience at a trade show is generally industry professionals. If this was a book trade show, then it would be commercial book buyers, librarians, etc. and the general public might not be invited, or might only be welcome on certain days. In the USA, there are currently over 10,000 trade shows held every year, and most of them have some sort of public option. Knowing your niche is key to doing well at these live events and being sure your book is on point for your market's expectations.

Other fairs and festivals. There needs to be an option on my list for shows in between the craft/maker events and trade shows. "Other fairs" are, well, *other fairs*. That might include county fairs, local town celebrations, sidewalk sales, music celebrations and concerts, and other events where various vendors might be welcome. I wanted to keep this option different from the others because the thing attracting a crowd is different. For these, attendees are *coming for the celebration or activity* rather than the shopping.

At these events, the mindset of the potential readers is not necessarily in buying mode, or if it is, it might be acutely focused on purchases related to the event. For example, maybe you have published an espionage thriller and decided to get a table at a regional gun show. Because there could be a strong overlap in the audience's interests, I daresay the genre might be a good fit there, but most people come to look at and/or purchase firearms, knives, and hunting equipment. On the one hand, a book might seem like an off the wall purchase, but a paperback is also a vastly smaller purchase than a new gun, and gun people are often readers as well. If they aren't, many have spouses who are. The *way* you pitch a book might shift with the audience's interests and you might talk about the guns your protagonist prefers and demonstrate knowledge here. It is a good way to hook a potential new reader.

Under this category would also be a good place to add themed festivals as well. That might include music festivals, car shows, renaissance festivals, and ethnic celebrations like Irish Fest or Oktoberfest. For these, you don't necessarily have to be laser focused on content. Pretty much anything can have its own festival.

Conventions. These are the big-themed shows that are my bread and butter. Their themes or niches can sometimes change or be multifaceted; a pop culture con might have a strong anime bent one year, and a strong sci-fi one the next. This is often due to whatever celebrity guests or special programs the organizers lined up for that year.

Some shows have taken on a life of their own so that you might attend a show without caring about what celebrities are there or what the theme is—though some of the audience might *only* care about the celebs or theme. GenCon is an example of that: many go to be in costume and spend time with friends and care very little for the fact that it is a convention specific to tabletop gaming. What is important is the *community*—and +80,000 like-minded people gathering together is a huge draw. Humans are built for community and peer interaction. Community might be what most differentiates a convention from other shows. I often use conference and conventions as interchangeable terms, but if I had to drill down into definitions, I'd note that conferences usually have a learning aspect to them with industry experts sharing their insights and conventions might have experts or not. (I've actually seen panels with two nerds on a stage yelling at each other to determine which Batman is the best Batman), but the conventions lean into the community as their chief identifier.

That community aspect, coupled with the theme, is what has produced such culturally unique things as cosplay and it has given us a whole subculture of nerddom that rivals professional sports (and folks walking around in their favorite player's jersey are really just cosplaying as athletes, if you think about it.)

Find your audience.

In addition to these types of events and using them as search terms or keywords as you use the internet to look for leads, you might also ask yourself where your target audience likes to go for events. Search for overlapping interest areas that your hypothetical target reader likes. This exercise is simple: just jot down things that he or she enjoys. Use these as search words and try coupling them with words such as convention, show, expo, conference, etc. and running them through a web search. It may turn up some events that were never previously on your radar.

Here's an example. Let's target the Amish Romance genre. Here is a list I came up with after a few minutes of thought:

Horseback riding
Mennonite colony
Quilting
Homesteading
Family
Religious
Homeschool
Craft
Country
Ranching
Holiday festivals

I threw that last one in because I've seen so many holiday-themed Amish romances and cozies that I thought it appropriate. Remember, we're looking for overlap … not only things that are directly relevant to Amish Romance. My character profile sheet from the earlier chapters is for a woman in her mid-40s who loves quilting and is curious about horseback riding and abandoning the suburbs to try homesteading. She has a couple of kids and has always homeschooled them for religious reasons.

Let's imagine the author lives in Tulsa, Oklahoma, and look for some events in a reasonable driving range. Within just minutes, I found:

8x Homeschool Conferences

6x Quilting shows

+90 craft and artisan shows

I only made a couple of searches and found over 115 different shows within reasonable driving distance of Tulsa, and only using "Conference" and "Convention" as a key term without dipping into trade shows, book clubs, etc. Granted, some of these might not be worth doing, but using this tactic will prove a powerful way to locate events where you can find readers.

Chapter Six: Tech

You Need Tech!

You need tech! (I wrote it twice because it's *that* important.)

I know that becoming an author is something often done later in life, when a person finally has time to commit to crafting their opus; that generation, currently, has some technology holdouts, folks who refuse to learn to use a computer and still think the internet is a passing fad. It's a stereotype that's not always true, but sometimes it is. It's relevant because I occasionally meet authors who are "cash only." There are enough out there that it is not uncommon to have a customer express surprise to learn that I take credit cards.

For consumer purchases, credit and debit cards are the most used form of payments and cash is actually the least used method of buying in the modern marketplace; only 19% of sales were cash, according to a 2020 survey. Of course, you never know how people will pay. Sometimes I'll do a show and have hardly any cash sales, followed by another with almost nothing else. Regardless, research by Dun & Bradstreet shows that people *spend* 12%-18% more when using credit cards.

Don't leave money on the table or create resistance to buying by not accepting the kinds of payments your customers want to use. I'm sure you scanned the last chapter's checklist and saw that I recommend a few pieces of technology. We'll talk about the items below and a few others, but in a different order.

- Credit Card Reader/point of sale
- Emergency power supply
- Apps installed on smartphone in case of problems with credit card reader
- Source of Wi-Fi, (such as hotspot capability)
- Alternative payment options
- Sales tax setup in point of sale

POS - Point of Sale

I'm assuming that you use a smartphone and are capable of navigating a few apps. Each application has a slight learning curve, so take your time exploring them. I am also going to teach the systems I regularly use. If you prefer a different setup, look for the principles and then apply them to your specific tech. For example, I use an android tablet, but maybe you prefer an iPad or your iPhone.

Your device could just be your smartphone, but I prefer to keep a wholly separate device for a variety of reasons and that is why I use a tablet. The first reason is that it's a cleaner setup. I'm also more likely to lose or break my cell since it goes everywhere with me. If I go to the restroom or to find food, I often have someone still running my booth/table and they can still take sales in my absence—the same is true if I get a phone call or important message that I have to get to in that moment. My business doesn't quit completely if my phone is tied up. For that reason, I am a huge fan of backups. My phone is also capable of running the same point of sale software/app (POS) and so I can have my booth help closing one transaction on one side while I'm doing the same on another.

The systems will sync and record all those sales together so I'm not having to track multiple sales accounts. It also syncs to my web store.

Making sure your phone has the same setup is vitally important. I could be traveling and meet someone completely random in the line for coffee. Learning that I'm an author, they might say, "I love Sci-fi! How can I buy your book?" You keep a few copies in your car everywhere you go, right? Right? *You should.* And being able to autograph a book and sell it on the spot will increase your likelihood of selling as well as your overall profit. I talked margins earlier. You'll make about ten dollars from that live sale versus about five from Amazon. And the likelihood they'll buy it later is low if an impromptu sales opportunity passes by. You're also more likely to turn that person into a super fan who will tell friends, "I met this cool author at Starbucks; you've got to check it out."

I mentioned web stores earlier. These things used to be expensive with monthly fees, setup hassles, security concerns, and were generally not worth it. But they were also a sign that an author was a legitimate business. Plus, I'd prefer to keep Jeff Bezos out of as many transactions as I can as a matter of preference. (I do respect the concerns of small brick and mortar bookstores.) My POS system integrates with a free bookstore feature that I have linked to my website so there exists a scenario where someone is buying a book from my website at the same time as I'm selling one on my mobile on one side of the booth and my wife is selling one from a tablet on the other side.

My POS tracks my inventory as well, so if I have only two copies on hand of my military space epic, Rendezvous at Havendell and we're each selling one, one of us won't be able to select and sell it. It will come back as Out of Stock. After any given show, I can look over my inventory and see what I need to order. It's better than the old way, which was to recount my entire collection after every show or keep (and regularly lose) a notebook recording my stock.

The POS app I use and prefer is Square (at squareup.com). It is free and they take a small percentage off each purchase, but I've found it to be my preferred app for the reasons I mentioned above. I can also save sales tax rates based on where a show is taking place and my online store will automatically add up my items' weight and add shipping on top. I simply package them and mail out each copy.

That brings up another topic: sales tax. Each show will have its own requirements based on the location. I write in *The Indie Author's Bible* and on my blog about how to get set up so you aren't paying tax twice on your products. You should always remember to add the sales tax on top of a sale. It is your obligation to collect it and it is your buyer's obligation to pay it. I hate taxes. *Hate.* I think they're immoral, unreasonable, and are a form of theft we've all been tricked into, frog-in-the pot style. But I pay them. Don't let your attitudes ever get in the way of business, and it's hard to attend book selling expos while in the clink.

I actually record *all* sales in my POS so that I can use it to track reports on how much I have to collect, report, and then remit to the government. That means I also use my POS on *cash sales*, which both deducts the items from my inventory tracker and keeps a record of the tax amount. It also means you can easily send a digital receipt if the buying party asks for one.

I'll write more about this when covering sales tactics, but when someone says, "Fifteen bucks?" and hands me a ten and five, I often eat the tax rather than arguing or asking. I keep a special percentage discount button set to the tax rate and press that to make the math even out and make sure the tax is still recorded that way. But if I'm ringing up the total and they're reaching for cash (or card) I always state the total as "$X.YZ after tax." People often think we either don't pay tax or are willing to entertain a little fraud because so many small-show authors' businesses are so small. Just remember, tax fraud is a crime. You will have to set up your paperwork with tax authorities far in advance of most shows and many events will require you to note your tax id number on the application, so look at your requirements early in the process.

Wi-Fi

Not all events have wireless internet available, and of those that do, many will charge you for access, especially the larger events. Many venues outsource their tech to an independent contractor, meaning added fees for services. Your POS will probably need access to the internet in order to process credit card transactions, and it's wise to never make assumptions. My wife sold a set of books recently at a show and handed the card back, but it hadn't finished processing due to spotty service (I regularly had to try 2 or 3 times), and the lady left with her books. The connection error caused my app to lock up and I had to reset the device, meaning I did not get paid for those two books. There is a spot on Square to record Loss, so the inventory remains correct.

My mobile phone can act as a hotspot, additionally, and I use this feature often. Some providers may include this for free, and others may charge for this additional service. Some people have to purchase additional hardware to have their own dedicated Wi-Fi and some people's home internet service providers even give this to customers who are often on the go. I believe it's worth having your own connection and I'm not a big fan of relying on other people's systems. I've done a lot of conventions where my booth neighbors ask me, "Is your internet connection slow, too?"

Come prepared and refuse to submit to the mercy of a bad or overloaded internet connection. My android tablet, which I run as my dedicated POS, has its own network signal for internet, but it is not as reliable as the hotspot on my cell and needs to be reset often. Always have a Plan B.

Another reason I prefer to have Wi-Fi available is for my newsletter sign-up page. Sometimes I can't get someone to buy, even though they are very interested. It might be due to money or available time, but whatever the reason, it is beneficial to sign them up on your newsletter/mailing list. You can even promise them that they'll get an ebook just for signing up and it'll be in their inbox before they leave the booth. (Newsletter Ninja will explain how to use automation tools to give away books and send an automated set of welcome messages to new subscribers without the need to do anything after setting it up). Maybe you just sold someone books and they seem on the verge of becoming your new super fan; get them on the mailing list.

But why do I need Wi-Fi for my mailing list sign-up?

I've seen a lot of my fellow authors hand a sheet of paper and a pen to have folks write down their addresses. I used to do this too. I found that I couldn't read most of them (is that an l, I, |, or 1?) It also made me sit down and type up a list and import it into my service. Instead, I purchased a very cheap android tablet on Black Friday and have it powered up and open to a browser with a few different tabs. Each tab will register them onto a different list and give the new subscriber a different, free ebook (this technique is called offering a reader magnet.) I just select the tab and hand over the device for them to input their own address. I keep on hand three tablets, one is my former POS which doubles as a backup in case my main one breaks or someone steals it (neither has ever happened, but it's worth being prepared), another is an older tablet someone gave me which is ok for browsing but too slow to run any meaningful apps, and the last is a Kindle Fire tablet I got for $20 on a Black Friday sale—this is my primary Newsletter Sign-up device.

A lot of authors want to run a giveaway and have prospective readers sign up on an entry ticket to be drawn for a free book later. I prefer the immediate sign-up with the device, and I've tested it for success. The ticket model means you still have legibility issues and extra work, you're also going to be out the cost of a book, and I've noticed that some people use it as an excuse to walk away. "Sorry, I'm not going to buy, but I *really* hope I win the giveaway." The dedicated NL tablet ensures you get people on the list with almost zero extra work and it also guarantees them a free book.

I should also say that a significant percentage of my most engaged NL readers came onto my list from meeting me at conventions and being on-boarded on the spot.

Websites

You really should have a website as an author. And no, having a Facebook page is not sufficient—social media is a whole different animal (and you don't own your traffic on social media. Facebook/Twitter/etc. does, and this will help insulate you from blow back and social media trolls.)

You don't need to be tech savvy to have a website. A lot of providers use WYSISWG (what you see is what you get), setups that are very user friendly and they have templates that will allow you to tweak a sample website with your own images and text or video content.

This is something you could play with endlessly, and you should do that. Maybe pick up a book specific to the topic. But start somewhere. And get your own website domain name. You may need to also get your own email to match it. For instance, my website is www.authorchristopherdschmitz.com and I have an email owner@authorchristopherdschmitz.com to match. Anti-spam laws have certain requirements on bulk email providers (you need one for your newsletter) such as Mailchimp and Mailerlite, both of which I have used. I now use the latter after outgrowing the first, but when I switched to Mailerlite, I had to use a professional email setup due to regulations. Wix, my website service provider, (who I have a love/hate relationship with, so don't consider that an endorsement), also provides that service. I *will* say that they are very user-friendly and Wix is a convenient choice even for tech-averse authors.

You can link your bookstore through your website as well. Go ahead and visit my website at the above link and click the Bookstore link in my header. I used to try keeping a blurb and image for all my books. Now, I use the bookstore that is part of my Squareup account and can sell books directly to folks. The sales are included on my Square reports, inventory, and ditto for taxes. Since I keep books on hand for my live events, I don't have to order from the printer and then wait. I keep enough supplies around for this (bubble mailers, boxes, and a tape gun) so that I can pack and ship them whenever an order alert hits my email. I also include an option for if the buyers want the book autographed. Yes, buyers pay a shipping fee, but if you are shipping in the USA and from the USA and it is only books, you have the option to use Media Mail which is vastly cheaper and includes a tracking number you can share with the purchaser. Every year I sell more books than the last via my online store and I did over $2,000 in sales from it last year, even though I feel like it is hardly utilized. The occasional sales do add up.

The most likely people to use my online bookstore are those who have already visited me at an event and who have my business card. Event visitors usually have the sense that artists and go-getters at conventions make better margins if they buy direct and are often happy to cut out the online distributor in favor of supporting an artist. Based on what I see selling on my website, I can also guess that these are mostly repeat customers who picked up a series starter elsewhere. The majority of my titles sold are books #2 and beyond in series.

You really do want to have a website. You should also have a newsletter sign-up option linked prominently on your website and it is a good practice to also have a pop-up box asking for it. Yes, those things are annoying, but they also work.

If all else fails, you can pay someone to build and/or manage your website for you. Include the link on every book's bio. Your social media page and newsletter sign-up links might change, but your website address is more likely to remain the same.

Apps you should pre-install

There's nothing worse than having unnecessary delays when your customer is ready to purchase. Every second that trickles by adds up to a bad result: a willing customer shrugging and saying,

"Oh well," and then walking away. If a transaction takes too much time to complete, this certainly might become the case.

I recommend having a digital wallet or P2P payment app set up already. This would include things like Venmo, Zelle, Cashapp, etc. Having a Paypal account is also a wise idea. You can link this to your credit or debit card if you like. Some shows that I have done, especially the smaller ones, will only take Paypal as their form of payment for a vendor fee.

These systems can also be used for payments, sometimes. It won't take the place of a credit card, but in emergency situations, they can come in handy. I once had someone who didn't have their wallet or cash and really wanted a book. He sent me the payment via Paypal and after I logged in through my Wi-Fi connection, I verified the money was there and signed his book. In another case, a 17-year-old girl who *loved* high fantasy and Dragonlance stopped at my comic con booth (a Tier 1 show). She had a prepaid card to limit her spending and about ten dollars left. I could have sold her the series starter and hoped she'd buy the rest, but she said she wanted all of what is currently an eight-book series. I asked if she had a parent at the convention or was here with friends. She decided to call her mother, who was at home, and arranged for her mom to Venmo me the money and she left with the whole set.

Remember that, if you *do* use that sort of alternative payment, still run it through your POS or your inventory will be off. I make a note of such transactions if they will involve a later bank transfer and run them through my POS as cash so that tax is collected and all my accounting and metrics remain more or less intact.

Square can, alternatively, take credit cards remotely as well. I could have had the mother read me the card numbers and details, or let the daughter type them, giving the mother some measure of security by not letting me type them in. Of course, I am at risk too, as I can't be certain that a card is not stolen under those circumstances and a P2P system is more secure.

I have had my Square cardreader malfunction and manually entered many credit cards or had to do the same with damaged cards that were unreadable. Square charges a higher fee for that, so be aware. If I am having hardware issues on my end, rather than ask the customer to wait and risk them saying, "I'll come back later and get it," which risks them, well, *not*, I will often manually enter the numbers. You can feel your way through that, but after trying two or three times to run a transaction, time stretches and things get uncomfortable.

Remember, if you're having issues, Roy and Moss of the IT Crowd highly suggest turning the machine off and back on again. If I've had any errors or issues and there is a slight lull, I'll do hardware and software resets right after.

Other Apps: Of course, there are a ton of other apps out there that will help you mitigate costs on your travels. I have used Getupside and Gasbuddy for fuel; the former will also give food local discounts. You will want a good GPS app to navigate you to unfamiliar places. I have used discount hotel finders and also Airbnb. While driving, if I am on my own, I will listen to audiobooks or author podcasts. Authors have to be readers, too, and this is a way to get in reading periods while driving. Otherwise, I feel like I've lost time when I could be writing or marketing.

Other Tech

Your devices are only good if they have power. Most events at Tier 3A and larger have a steep up-charge if you need electricity. This is usually due to contracts with the Venue and their power supplier. I try to manage my power the best I can and charge my tools overnight. Still, it is wise to carry one or two battery/charger packs to resupply your energy in case your card reader or POS needs it. If you lose all your power, your entire purpose for being at the show is drastically reduced.

I try to make sure that everything I'm going to rely on has a battery option. Some of the shows I vend at have no access to power, even if I wanted it. There are a lot of outdoor festivals where getting electricity is downright impossible, so be sure to do your diligence as you research what you'll need for each show.

Christopher D. Schmitz

Chapter Seven: What Do I Need

By now, there is likely an event or two that you're considering doing. What will you need to have prepared to succeed?

When you arrive at this live event, you're going to need printed materials that fall into two categories. These items *do not* include the books themselves. Most commercial printers do not specialize in book printing. Even if your work is a magazine or in a comic book format, you will still be best served by a specialty printer for those. There is a need for your local printer, but you will probably go broke trying to print your product there. A local printer was very excited when I had them print a single demo comic for me that I needed for a show and didn't have time to wait for mail service via my regular comic printer. They'd hoped I could get my $5 promotional comic book from them in the future and promised they could get my cost aaaaallllll the way down to $15 per comic (not a typo). I asked if he was familiar with math as he didn't realize how bad a deal it was to give away an item that cost me $15 in the hope that someone miiiiiiggghhhtt buy a $15 book next.)

The items you will need will fall into the following categories: materials to help sell now and materials to help you sell later. While I know many of you own a printer at home and will be tempted to print slap together some materials on your own with your home setup, I highly advise that you get some professional creative help. You can hire design work at low cost on Fiverr.com (a freelancing website) and I also encourage you to use your local print shop for this. There is a noticeable quality difference in what your local printer can make versus what you can produce at home. This will be noticed by shoppers and you want every aspect of your display items to feel professional. Home printers scream DIY. The more professional your setup feels, the easier it will be to make sales.

Materials to help sell now
I keep a few price sheets at my table to advertise both the cost of books and also the cost of buying a series. I do not give special pricing except when someone buys multiple books; I sell a few different book packages, usually specific to a series. I will give more details later.

My first rule of sales is this: a person can't buy from you if they don't see you. I used to run a massive fundraiser for a nonprofit where we'd sell fruit out of a semi-truck trailer for 5-10 days. It was our single biggest annual fundraising event. One year, our local Wal-Mart manager, who loved what our nonprofit was about, offered to let us use their parking lot since they were the highest-traffic business in the community. I jumped at the chance, and it was only about a half-block move from our previous location. Then I fielded many phone calls from people who simply could not find us... I remember one conversation:

Buyer: I don't see you—I've looked everywhere and you're not at Wal-Mart.

Me: I assure you I'm right here. In fact, I see you. You're looking right at me.

Buyer: No. I can't find you!

Me: Walk East. I'm literally right there. You're only forty yards away. I'm the guy waving his arms and jumping up and down.

What happened is that our trailer looked like every other trailer in the parking lot. Even though ours had a bunch of colorful banners on it, people could not differentiate between the trailers because the banners faded into the background. Our location became practically invisible. They "couldn't see the forest for the trees."

You need to have a booth setup that makes you visible, and to do that you'll want some signage to help you stand out, even if you don't get the ideal placement that puts you where you can stand out. I have a ten-foot backdrop with bright colors and I also use a table skirt. All of that has branding on it to let people know, at a glance, what I'm about.

Additionally, I have half a dozen 3' wide and 6' tall retractable banner stands. Within seconds, I can set up whichever ones I think will best fit my event and appeal best to the audience of any given event.

Materials to help sell later

I have had bookmarks printed in the past. Additionally, I have had flyers, posters, and business cards. These each have varying degrees of efficacy, but the business cards are an absolute must. You also have to know how to use them: a business card that gets thrown away in short order fails to do its job, and most business cards fall into that category.

Because so many business cards get tossed, I often wonder if they are a good investment for so many authors. When I've run out in the past, I usually tell people to take a picture and then look up my books online and wonder about some form of digital business card. I know I've tossed a lot of business cards in my day and found that they have almost the same value as a bookmark. It can hold a page, but rarely gets looked at or thought about. That's why I don't keep bookmarks on hand anymore. It's provided no value for me as a seller.

But I have learned the trick to business cards and have had people meet me at a show who pull out the business card they got from me a year or more previously and hundreds of miles away. Your card stands a reduced chance of being trashed if it is either so helpful that it won't get thrown, or it is so clever that it is kept. I know some marketing folks insist on putting a business partner's coupon or discount on the back. The challenge in the literary world is to find something that is useful enough to be kept and provide value in any geographic region you might visit. And then you run into a different problem. There's an old adage that "what you win people with is what you win them to," and in this case, it means that a hypothetical taco coupon on the back of your card holds more value to the holder than your book info.

My card is clever. Because I identified my reader niche as an avid consumer of nerd culture, I have them printed double-sided and made it up to look very similar to a fully playable Magic the Gathering card. It directs people to my website and to my mailing list and has my photo on it. I keep a second, more professional business card with my direct contact information on it for networking purposes and for people I am consulting with or who want to talk about bringing me to a con as a guest or bring me in to speak at their event. Not every person gets that card, as I prefer to interact with most people at my own discretion and timeline via email. Four A.M. phone calls to talk about my character's motivations are something I'd prefer to avoid.

I don't do much with posters, although I've done some in the past. But I do carry a stack of half-page flyers that I've made up. My best-selling comedy book (a murder mystery at comic con) has a lot of tongue in cheek pseudo-potty humor while managing to remain PG13. Taking the jokes one step further, I usually hang a few of these above the urinals in the men's rooms and in toilet stalls to entertain captive audiences. I use a sharpie to mark my booth number and have had people come to buy straight away after reading it. Again, like the business card, it has to be clever and have a strong hook. You should also make sure it's not against con rules. Some prohibit hanging any signage by tape or any sticky substance. Some prohibit certain kinds of tape, so know where the line is and carry multiple kinds of tape and hangers.

Remember that printed materials have a cost and if they don't demonstrate that they are bringing in a return for you, feel free to ditch that particular marketing effort. Some ideas work for some people and won't work for others. Feel free to emulate the things other writers use, but also don't feel that you have to have postcards just because a few other authors have them. Use what works, ditch the rest, and just because you think an idea is amazing, if your readers don't also think so, then keep refining what you're doing until everything clicks.

Product

You obviously need the books that you plan to sell. Where should you buy them and how much stock should you keep? Can you dropship them?

I'm going to address these questions in reverse. Sometimes dropshipping (having your products sent to your sales location from the production/distribution warehouse,) is an option. I dropshipped a big load of books to an event to reduce some of my travel concerns. I'd done the event before, a large comic book convention in Missouri, and so I knew about what I would sell. I made an order and had the books delivered to my uncle who lived near there. And then, two weeks before the event, the nationwide COVID shutdown hit. Not only did I lose the event, but I had lots of product floating around in another state that I could not access, even if I wanted to or could somehow sell them locally.

That is not an illustration to tell you to avoid dropshipping. I just want to demonstrate that any time you add one more ball to the ones you're juggling, you might get unexpected results. I should also mention that many events organize freight shipping for a fee, so you may not need a local contact to receive your shipments. For example, some of the conventions I do all share the same promoting company and they can take your products from one location to another on the circuit so it is ready for your arrival at a later event, storing it securely in the interim. I don't use this personally, but many people do who sell other miscellaneous items. I do know there are other shipping options that will allow you to mail packages to yourself in other locations and if you check with a hotel, often they can receive a package which you can collect during your stay; you will want to make prior arrangements with the lodging manager.

One thing to keep in mind is that you may have different tax obligations if you do this. When I ship books to myself in my home state, I have a tax exemption on file with the printer, so my books are tax free to me and then I pay sales tax on the sale price. Without that, I will be forced to pay sales tax twice. Those exemptions are set up state to state and you will want to be fully aware the nuances. If I have Amazon/KDP print $500 worth of books for me ($5 each, which I will sell for $15 each) and I don't set this up, I will have to pay an extra $40 in sales tax on that $500 invoice, and then pay another $120 to the tax office after those books sell for a total tax obligation of $160. That first $40 should have been $0 since I am technically a resale business and not a customer. The other $120 was additional monies collected at the point of sale and was never mine to begin with, but that $40 *was mine*, and those tax bills add up over time. If I ship books to an out-of-state area and I don't have my paperwork recorded with the printer, they will have to charge me the additional tax. Sometimes it is unavoidable, but there is a process to get around wasting money in almost every situation. Cutting avoidable expenses is just as good as making more profit when it comes to your bottom line. Just remember to get your tax paperwork done far enough in advance. I always recommend you do this early in your author career to maximize your savings, but I realize most authors put this off until they are ordering more than a handful of books at a time.

How much stock is it best to keep on hand? I aim for a few more than I think I can sell during a great show. I've had a few sellout events which made me puff up my chest as I called my wife afterward. She pointed out that I had just lost potential money. "You won't even know what you didn't sell because you were out of books. You might have sold another fifty books, which would have been an extra $500 ... you should start bringing more stock." And she was absolutely right. (Get yourself a pessimist if you're an optimist, or vice versa, if needed. They'll keep you balanced.)

Since we're talking about margins and bottomline pricing, let's talk about quality and print costs. It may surprise you to find that my highest quality printer is my cheapest option. However, the printer, Baker and Taylor, is not POD so I had to order over a thousand copies and arrange freight shipping. Doing so meant first having a plan to sell that many copies of one particular title and having a storage solution for a half-pallet of books. Of the most common options, the next highest quality is IngramSpark, followed by KDP Print (formerly Createspace,) which is the Amazon-owned print shop. There are others out there, and they vary greatly in quality, but these three are the most consistently used and endorsed by me, and most indies with whom I've crossed paths. And, like buying generic label food, they actually handle a lot of the backend work for other companies. (For instance, IngramSpark handles the printing solutions for DrivethruRPG, although the website and distribution is different.)

As far as POD goes, I get the best print price on paperbacks that I sell from KDP Print and so 90% of my copies that are produced POD are from there. My non-POD title is still my best seller at live events and that is why I made a significant investment into it upfront so I can make a bigger pay-off long term. For the POD options, KDP also gives me a more consistent shipping rate. As long as I make reasonable-sized orders I can keep my shipping costs at around 50 cents per book (which means I'm usually ordering 120+ total books at a time. They can be mixed titles, but more books usually means lower costs, though I haven't gotten that number lower than 40 cents in years and shipping rates change frequently.)

Ingramspark (IS) has an option at checkout that shows you the number of boxes per crate (the max of a title that can fit into a box.) It may be an error at Ingramspark, but for the past couple of years, making an individual order with more than one crate has done wild things to the shipping charges; sometimes putting multiple books into a crate can have the same effect. I find shipping at a reasonable price on a crate, and then double the amount of books, but the shipping would triple, or even more, meaning I'd have to make multiple, separate orders to keep my costs reduced by making two or three duplicate orders in order to prevent the shipping from going crazy.

Their customer service is also garbage. I would never say this if I did not mean it. IS support used to be very good, but then they completely removed the customer service option except for the ability to send an email that will take days or weeks to get a response, if at all. (I kid you not, I just got an email response saying they are working on something I asked about more than a year ago—and they did not even resolve the issue.) It is actually easier to get support from KDP/Amazon.

In the interest of providing data here that may be relevant to printing and pricing, I made an order of one crate of books at IS, which was 32 books. The shipping came down to $65.62 which is more than $2 per book and remember that shipping comes out of your profit margins. Those 32 copies at KDP cost me $19 to ship, or 59 cents each. At $4.53 each, IS also costs more per copy than KDP, which was $3.61. After IS's fees, the total was $212.57 versus KDP's $134.52 for the same, or a savings of $2.43 *per book* at KDP. It's hard to argue with that math when you're trying to be profitable.

So why even use Ingramspark? Besides the fact that I think Jeff Bezos might be the anti-Christ, there are several reasons to choose IS despite the cost differential. I use both services. I do a fair amount of business overseas in European countries and in Australia and New Zealand where IS is more competitive, and the shipping is actually much reduced. IS also has much better print quality, despite a lighter weight paper (which makes their USA shipping rates absurd since one would think the rates would be reduced), and their shipping is also qualitatively better. (I don't know if it's worth the +300% price tag, but it *is* better). I've received a large number of boxes from IS and though their speed is slower than KDP, my books are always packed well enough to prevent shipping damages and bending. I've had a lot of mangled paperbacks and other weird shipping anomalies through KDP's systems. On the quality front, IS's inks are darker, and their covers' lamination is better. I've done outdoor shows and noticed that on hot and humid days the pages, and especially the covers, of KDP books will curl in a much more pronounced fashion than the IS equivalent.

Another reason is that IS offers some products that KDP does not. While KDP now offers hardcovers, if you want your POD book to have a dust jacket, you will have to use IS as KDP doesn't offer that at the time of writing this guide, likewise with some advanced options for colored print pages. There are some additional options you have access to with IS if your book is in color or within certain page counts.

If you want to have copies available to sell *before* your release date, you will need to purchase those books through a non-KDP printer and IS has a good track record of doing this for me. If your book's release date has not yet arrived on Amazon, you will only be able to order them in batches of five and they will be branded with a "not for resale" banner printed over the cover. That may impact your book release plans if you hoped to have a live event on launch day.

But the main reason I use IS is one I mentioned earlier in the book. If selling at an event that includes libraries or bookstores in competition with Amazon, you must not have a KDP ISBN. I should mention that you *can purchase* an ISBN separately and then use KDP to print your book with your own imprint data, thereby avoiding the ISBN/Amazon cross-contamination.

There is one more thing I want to recommend, and I've helped walk other authors through the math on this. If you write books in a series, you really should carry omnibus editions. Research shows that readers love to binge books just as much as viewers love to binge television shows. Most marketing advice pertinent to indies is to harness read-through to get readers to purchase your whole series as quickly as possible.

What if you could make it easier for the reader to do that while you also made more money? I'm going to show you how.

I sell trilogy editions of my different series books. Each one is a monstrous tome that includes all the books, and I'll often include a few extra bonuses. I sell these at a reduced rate versus buying the books at a discounted bundle, and so that helps sway buying decisions.

Here's the breakdown, using KDP rates (not including shipping), and using a trilogy which I no longer carry on my table but sell only via my website or at specific events where I know it will have a ready market. (This was my first series ever written, and my modern writings are just so much better, have more reviews, and have more active reader bases.)

I sell books 1-3 individually for 16.99 each. They are large fantasy books, averaging about 115,000 words per story. It's $50.97 for a customer to buy them individually. I offer a steep discount and sell them for $42 if they buy all three at my booth at the same time ($9 off). At $42 to buy, they cost $15.86 to print for a profit of $26.14. I'm making roughly $8.71 per book, even after discounting.

I sell the trilogy omnibus as one fat book about as big as KDP's systems can assemble (it's over 800 pages and has a larger trim size) and I sell it for $39.99. The omnibus costs $10.79 to print since there are not additional covers printed and it is based on how the system calculates the cost per page ... it allows authors to find a kind of spongy groove to fall into which lets us make some extra money per book based on the mathematic formula. The profit is $29.21, or $9.74 per book.

I even do a little better with my other series. You can manipulate your prices and discounts to capitalize here. Buyers, knowing they are likely to binge the whole set, will often gravitate to the lower price. The books that I still sell out of are the omnibus sets. Because it's still more likely that I'll sell just the series starter, I carry many copies of book #1 and a bunch of omnibus editions, and then a smaller collection of books #2 and later in any given series. Even when I sell out of the omnibus edition, I can still sell through the series with the books sold individually and as bundles without having to carry a much larger amount of overhead by bringing a huge stock of omnibuses. It also helps create a sense of urgency that comes with limited supply when you get down to just a few omnibus editions. The flexibility indies have with pricing is a big part of the supplemental material about pricing and it is available as a free download.

Other supplies

Tech gadgets are great. We talked about the importance of your POS and having a secure form of storage for your cash is important (a money box or deposit bag). You may or may not bring your own food and opt to bring a cooler. I always bring plenty to drink in mine because I know how raspy my voice will get if I don't keep it lubricated, and I'm keenly aware of my caffeine addiction. Most shows will have drinks available for vastly inflated prices (I've seen black drip coffee for a dollar an ounce, which is insane). I only drink sugar-free soft drinks, of which most vendors only carry an extremely limited variety and so I bring my own. Comfortable shoes are also a necessity since you'll be on your feet most of the day.

Despite those preferences, there are two other items that I'd hate to be caught without. The first one is a collapsible cart/wagon. I picked one up for about $75 and it folds into a self-contained package only slightly larger than one box of books. The wagon reduces my load in time and my exit/tear down time by a significant margin.

The second is my booth's supply kit. I carry my cash box, print materials, book stands, and other booth supplies in a large, wheeled suitcase. In it, I keep a variety of random items that have come up on occasion and I keep enough supplies to be able to share with other vendors in need. Here are some of the things I keep in there:

A variety of binder clips
Four different kinds of tape
Flashlight
Chain
String
Thumbtacks
Safety pins
Rubber bands
Pens and markers
Spare drop cloths
Paper
Hand sanitizer and other PPE
Spare change bag
Zip ties
Plastic food utensils
Bags
A spare credit card reader and charger
Batteries
Ibuprofen

Screwdrivers

Sticky notes

Spare printed copies of my tax paperwork

Folding book display stands

Emergency kit

Booth emergency supply kit: knife, clear and painter's tape, chain, pins, clips, sharpies, etc.

Chapter Eight:
In the Booth Part 1
(Attitude and Tactics)

Everything up until now has been prep work and physical systems. Now we're shifting into tactics, and the first thing is to keep expectations and frustration out of your head.

Attitude

Attitude is everything for you. It will make or break you. You're going to hear a lot of "No-thank-you's," though they might not be quite so overt. People who aren't ready to buy will often just say, "Thanks," and then walk away. That's called a soft no. *And that is not a hard no.* A hard no means they are definitely not returning. But sometimes soft no's will come back.

When I worked for the national sales team I mentioned before, we were trained in making high-pressure sales. Most of the tactics shared in this book are similar—except for the parts about being pushy with the close. We were taught, and it was true, that people who you didn't close on the spot would never return—even if they said, "I've got to finish what I came here for and I'll stop before I leave." The product was expensive and so people would reconsider once they were gone. Many would use that as a form of a soft no, which is a passive way of asking, "please don't force me to directly, actually, say 'no.'" People who hate confrontation do this all the time—they'd rather let down someone's hopes than use binary oppositional language. Less than half of one percent of people who said, "I'll come back for it," ever returned.

Here is the good news for authors at live events: something like 60-80% of those who promise to return really do so. In tracking these numbers, it is closer to the higher end of that percentage. A lot of them don't want to carry a book at a big event which might have some hands-on interaction and if the event is a comic convention, like where I vend, they may have costume props to deal with or be planning on celebrity photo ops and want to keep their hands free. Having bags helps reduce this somewhat, though I rarely keep bags with me except a nicer printed kind which I use as giveaways for some up-selling tactics. Larger Tier 3 shows and bigger ones often have branded bags that they give away at the gate to encourage spending, and some events that I do ban plastic bags for one reason or another, so I rarely worry about it. One way I help mitigate the risk of a non-returner is to offer to keep their purchase behind the table for them.

"I only have so many copies when I travel to shows and I'd hate to run out of the book you want. If you want to ring these up now, I'll autograph them all while you're gone and have them ready for you to pick up when you come back." That often works, especially if the buyer is purchasing more than one book, which makes lugging a book stack around the event an obvious inconvenience for them.

All the above is to say, don't let a soft 'no' get you down. When I do a show, I try to engage as many people as I can. Every interaction, even the no's, are meaningful—if nothing else it opens the opportunity for them to hear about your writing. I mentioned last chapter that they can't buy from you if they don't see you. They might look at your booth but not really see it unless you invite them to interact, so brush off the annoyance of a non-sale and keep talking to people. If you let frustration win, you will be unable to sell.

Nobody sells by sitting back, keeping away from the table, and wearing a frown. We all feel like Grumpy Cat sometimes, especially after a particularly difficult interaction—yes, sometimes people will directly insult you. It probably has more to do with them than it does with you unless you've intentionally provoked them somehow, but some people are also just miserly asshats who only feel a sliver of joy by spreading the malaise they suffer from. I have shrugged when people have been jerks and told them directly to their face, "You could have just told me, 'I don't know how to read.'" Tit for tat, but with a little humor. Then again, I don't mind confrontation and I'm more than willing to throw a crap sandwich back at the waiter who delivered it … escalating anger brings me amusement, at least, and I'll have fun with anyone with violent reactions to reading. But that's my personality and I'm not above some carney-style heckling. I've made more than a few people laugh and come back to actually buy books. You don't have to do any of this, but you do have to find a way to let negativity roll off of you, reset, and engage the next person. Maybe it takes you a few minutes or a sip of Proper Twelve; whatever you need to do, don't let someone else's attitude rob your joy and profits.

Attitude might be the hardest part to master because it's something you have to do and constantly maintain. It's not something that is accomplished just by knowing, it can only be achieved by *being*. And *being* is much harder than *knowing* or even by *doing*, and intentionally *being* is only truly achieved by also *knowing* and *doing*. Once you establish a track record of success at events, however, the *being* comes easier because you know you can expect the reward: sales and readership.

You've got to want to make the sales and earn the readership. That motivation will help drive you to success. If you do everything in this book, but can't get the attitude part under control, no number of clever sales tactics will get you where you want to be and you'll struggle.

Since claiming I'd talk about tactics, I've written a thousand words about attitude, but it's integral to reset our thinking. Most people's idea of being an author is a little like being rich. We're in love with the idea of "having arrived," but few of us are willing to do the work required to get there. Some people quit the author business after starting a manuscript (or even before), and some quit after their book(s) are produced. I've seen it: people sitting six feet back from their table, staring at their cell phone and making zero effort to engage. I was at the largest literary show in my state a few years back running the publishers' booth for a traditional company I was signed with at the time. The guy opposite our table sat just as described above. Maybe one or two people stopped and had to practically force him to engage; the author seemed like he was inconvenienced by them. He made zero sales through the event and left early. I've seen that happen at several shows, and this isn't only an author/artist problem, either. But we creators have an idea that we should be basking in the accolades of our fans ... and that's an expectation that is going to cause you frustration.

That is why you've got to *want* to sell books, not just be famous—because the latter is a goal with no chartable path. You'd be better off playing the lottery.

Here's the harsh truth: nobody is attending the show to see you, unless your mom is coming—and I've actually got advice about that later.

You have to make yourself relevant to the present audience. I have a small handful of folks who come to a show looking for me now, but only because I've hustled to make some fans. (By this, I mean that coming to see me is a deciding factor on whether or not they attend the show.)

The good news is that *being* that person folks come to see is a possibility. Start selling and work the process. Once you start, it may take a while to get moving, but you can only go up from zero.

We'll move into tactics and pragmatic "how to" advice now. If you follow the below advice, *and* your signage/visibility is good, and you are at an event where your target audience is the focus, then you will sell well. If all those things are good and you are selling poorly, then attitude is likely your sticky wicket.

How to Sell Basics

1. Look for ways to engage and be ready to engage. I mentioned the guy who sat back from his booth and did not pay attention. You should be close enough that folks associate you with your table. I take several steps back when I'm grabbing a snack or need a moment. That is enough of a cushion that folks perceive the space as a signal for "don't engage." A space cushion is an effective enough deterrent. If I am eating lunch, but still close enough to touch my table (and my table/signage looks appealing) folks will stop and engage me even if I am stuffing my face. But don't rely on your marketing materials or a passive approach. Watch browsers' eyes as they grow close—if the eyes linger on your covers, become a human pop-up ad. Greet the customer in that split second. Once it has passed, so has your best opportunity.

2. Don't sit. I mentioned comfortable shoes earlier. You might also consider an anti-fatigue mat. I don't want to carry extra stuff and so I suffer, but it may be important to you. Whatever you can do to be on your feet, do it. "Nobody sells from a chair," is a phrase I've heard before. It's not entirely true, but it *is* easier to engage from a standing position. Plus, if you start the sale from a chair and have to stand (and some tactics further in this chapter will necessitate mobility) the standing carries a psychological connotation that the buyer has inconvenienced you, and that creates resistance to the sale and encourages a buyer to disengage before

you get them to the POS. Anything you can do to decrease resistance to the sale helps you succeed.

3. Attitude. Did I talk about this yet? I often jokingly say, "Drink if you have to." This is less about the attitudes I covered above and more about putting on an extrovertative (I just made up that word) front. If you are an introvert, pretend you are an extrovert. It is key to engaging. Pretend they are part of your book. Pretend you are someone else. Get jacked up on pixie sticks and caffeine. Whatever your method, you will need to burn emotional energy in your booth. Just make it happen. Plan for it. Get lots of sleep the nights before any sale days and the nights after—but being an author, and getting people to be your readers, is work. Regardless of what you've heard, nothing about this business equals free money.

4. Discriminate, but also don't. We covered this earlier in the relationships chapter. Look for points of connection to engage. Maybe they are wearing a Doctor Who shirt and you happen to have a life-sized TARDIS in your front yard. (At the peak of Who's popularity, that was the case for me.) If they're wearing a shirt for a band you like, use that as an entry point of conversation. If there is a fandom connection you can trace to your book, *use it!* "I love your Firefly shirt—I'm actually a contributor to the expanded Firefly universe and write a series that's the next best thing to getting a Season 2." Just don't lie, but embellishments are acceptable. The previous line is one I often use for my Dekker's Dozen series; I contributed game modules to the Galeforce 9 Firefly game Brigands and Browncoats.

If two people are walking close and one person appears to be a member of your target audience and the other does not, I focus my energy on a split-second gut-call. However, I try to ensure my opening pitch will be loud enough that both people can hear. I've been wrong and sold to person #2. It happens, but you've got to make the call and establish eye contact with one of them.

5. Have your elevator pitch nailed down. I pitch my books as a series and, for most of them, have both a high-concept pitch and a movie trailer pitch. Both are short, succinct and have been refined over many pitches based on what works. "Think of this series like a female Percy Jackson character versus Cthulhu ... and there's werewolves." If the person is male, I'll usually leave off the gender identifier. Another high concept pitch I use: "Shadowless is like I Am Legend meets City of Ember." If the look on their face shows that they don't know either or both in that pitch, I'll launch into my second pitch to explain. "Only a few hundred humans remain alive in an underground facility surrounded by miles and miles of subterranean tunnels that are lit by bright light panels. They are all deathly afraid of the dark ... and what lives in the shadows—the monstrous thing that wiped out humanity on E-day: Extinction Day ... and now, something is making the lights go out and that ancient evil has found a way *inside*." Author comparisons are also helpful. "If you like Stephen King, Shadowless is right up your alley ... a dark and scary alley."

6. Ask for a connection point. This is helpful if you need to change things up or have had trouble finding a way "in." You can always ask, "What kinds of stories do you like," I always clarify, "including TV shows, movies, video games, or other mediums?" I often open with this question. But be prepared for them to either not know or answer with "Basically everything." To which I usually joke around with something like a very loud greeting, "Finally, someone else who enjoys Erotic Teletubbies Fan fiction as much as I do!" Then again, one of my best-selling books is derivative pop culture comedy, so I can get away with it. Probably a bad line if this is an event in your local church basement. But you can continue to ask refining questions until you zero in on a landing point. What you're looking for is the best way to engage them with your book. At one point or another, you need to turn the corner from a conversation *about them* to a conversation *about your book*. If all

else fails, simply ask, "Can I tell you about my book(s)?" They'll give you a yes or no answer and you can respond accordingly.

7. Assume every sale is a cold sale. This means you recognize they didn't come here to buy a book from you today. They might even claim to not be a reader, or to be bad at it. You have to be prepared to overcome objections. If they are still talking to you, they are still a potential customer. They just have a few concerns you need to get out of the way first:

Q-I used to love reading.

A—>Why did you quit? (Give a list of reasons why you read.)

Q-I just don't have any time.

A—>Have you ever tried audiobooks? 90% of my books are available and I love to listen to audiobooks especially while I am commuting.

Q-I'm not good at reading/have a disability.

A—>Have you ever tried audiobooks? 90% of my books are available and that's helped a lot of folks in similar situations. If you'd like, you can take a picture of any of my covers, so you remember which title to search for in an audio bookstore.

Q-I only read on my e-reader.

A—>I mean, I can autograph the screen of your Kindle with a sharpie, but it's going to make reading more difficult.

Q-I've already got too many books to read.

A—> But we all know the rules. Autographed books go to the top of the pile.

Q-It's not really my genre.

A—>An autographed book makes a great, thoughtful gift. I can personalize it for whomever … plus you can preview it that way and see if it's something you might like, too.

Q-I only watch TV shows.

A—>Have you ever heard someone say, "The book was better?" If you read, you'll get the story well before it's made into a movie or Netflix special, and if everybody stopped reading, there wouldn't be any new shows. Plus, I'd love an autographed copy of the book that my favorite movies were made from ... maybe this book could be that for you.

There are lots of ways to overcome objections. You'll get strange excuses on the fly, but most of them will be variations on common ones such as those above.

8. Dress for the crowd, if relevant. I often dress in superhero costumes at comic conventions. If I was writing about fishing, I'd dress like a pro angler while at an Outdoor Sports Expo or like an Amish maiden if I wrote themed romance (though I wouldn't shave my beard). Remember, it's less about fitting in, it's about showing that you respect the interests of the target audience and creating an instant connection. If you do this, do it well. It's completely optional but can add a layer to your engagement attempts and visibility.

9. Ask for the Sale. Just like there is a soft no and a hard no, there is a soft ask and a hard ask. A soft ask leaves some wiggle room so you can continue to dispel resistance to a purchase if he or she isn't quite ready to buy yet, but a hard ask is binary, and a negative response kills any future ask. That is why I usually lead with a soft ask if I think I can still get them to make a purchase. Sometimes, with difficult people, I'm ready to be done and move on to someone who I can sell to and so I want a yes or no so I don't waste time. This is usually with someone who is either combative but still willing to look at your books, someone with an ulterior motive (they're really looking for a way to sign you up for their MLM scheme and are willing to listen to your book pitch first), or they're a booth barnacle. I'll discuss those later.

A soft no asks "will you buy this?" without using those words and looks like this:

-I accept cash or credit card. [Pause and wait for a response.]

-Can I autograph or personalize these for you?

-Here is the price list, but I also offer a multi-book discount on the bundles listed right here.

-I'm ready whenever you are.

-So which books are you taking home today?

A slightly harder ask is, "Can I ring that up for you?" even if you get a "no" and people begin to depart, I'll offer them a free ebook if they have any interest. That way they can see if they like my books before making a purchase. I'll write more about this in the next chapter.

10. Be a good booth neighbor. The person(s) adjacent to you is in the trenches alongside you. They are facing the same challenges you are, and so you'll want to remember that they are your allies. Don't steal from your allies. If they are engaging a customer, don't try to take their people. It's rude and will cause resentment. Sometimes cross-selling is unavoidable, and hopefully your neighbors are not insecure or the jealous type, but if you can avoid directly poaching customers, that will build good future relations. That is also a reason I try to not be directly adjacent to other authors: it helps lessen jealousy to a degree, among other reasons. If customers wander away from your neighbors and come to you, it is perfectly acceptable to engage them, but don't interrupt your neighbor or try to steer their customers to your booth instead of theirs.

Your booth neighbor will often be willing to watch your table for you while you run to use the restroom, hit up a food vendor, or stretch your legs and do some brief sightseeing/shopping. Be willing to reciprocate and engage with them in your downtime. I've made many friends on convention circuits, especially with folks who do as many shows as I do. It can even lead to future networking and advice on which shows are the best producing and collaboration/info sharing that can help you take your game to the next level.

Chapter Nine:
In the Booth Part 2
(Selling)

Selling is a lot like writing. It connects a need with an appropriate answer. This concept is easier to understand if you write nonfiction, but it is true with fiction, too, except that with fiction the questions look like, "How do I escape real life into a world with XYZ?" The most difficult part is discerning what XYZ is for any given reader, but that is why we did our best in previous chapters to identify our readers. With non-fiction, it might look like, "How can I sell more books at live at events?" *Well* ... have I got a book for you.

Still, fiction does also meet a need. The trick is in finding a way that your book (which is your answer), fits into a mold that meets the buyers' needs (desire for knowledge, escape, etc.) If you can do that, you can make a sale.

This chapter will deal with the practical steps and techniques to closing a deal and will build on the contents of the last chapter while also adding in some additional tricks and tips. And truth be told, it's great to remind even myself of what I do, how I do it, and why. In fact, I'm at a convention while I write these words. I would highly recommend against trying to write while in your booth or you'll look like you'd rather be anywhere else.

How to Sell

There is a reason why we talked about relationships and building connections *first*. All the preceding contents build into these:

1. Greet people. Say hello, wave, put your general dorkiness on display. Do something to try to open a dialogue. "I love your shirt... Do you like to read...? How did you get all those extra chins?" Maybe not that last one, but you get the point. This is the part that introverts struggle with: initiating a new connection from a cold start. For this to be effective, you also have to be able to maintain eye contact. If you are at a comic convention and choose to wear a costume, make sure it does not conceal your face. During the post-COVID conventions at mask-mandated shows, I tested my theory that people have to be able to see sincerity on your face as you pitch your books. *You have to believe that people will enjoy your book, or their BS detector will activate.*

I already knew to avoid face coverings after comparing sales from shows where I wore a full-face costume versus one where you could see my face. Open face outperformed by a significant margin. My wife purchased an additional shield system that covers the face behind clear plexi. (Elementary teachers understand that young children need to see mouth shapes during reading.) I used that at mask-mandated shows. My sales improved as much as they could despite the reduced post-pandemic crowds.

2. While pitching, place a physical book in your prospect's hands, turning it over so he or she can read the rear blurb and see the

price tag. This helps them feel a sense of ownership already. It's an old but effective psychological trick: they will have to hand the book back if they are not interested.

With many buyers, even in the post-COVID world, I notice a reluctance to take something in hand. Rather than let it get awkward if they don't want to acknowledge you are trying to hand them something, I merely put it down, cover side up. Some people recognize it as a sales tactic (or even as a soft-sell/soft-ask) and those people sometimes take it as an opportunity to disengage and leave, freeing you up to shrug and then pitch the next person. *Others*, however, who have a fear of touching will bend closer and read the book where it lies, and that is perfectly ideal for keeping engaged.

In the Amazon age, people are used to reading blurbs before making decisions, so it keeps in line with expectations, but a reader who returns the book is signaling a kind of soft no. Still, people will feel more inclined to buy something once they have it in hand. I can't give you hard data on it, but I believe it is true. Also, it will give you a chance to demonstrate the professional quality and nature of your book, which will also help you move copies.

3. Which book do I try to sell? "What book is your favorite book?" is a question asked of me often, especially at smaller shows where there is more time to spend with a customer. For me, and I assume this is true for any author, the book I am most excited about is the one that I am currently writing. My *best* book is one that I spent the most time on and has the most of myself in its characters. The one that sells the best is a different one again. The one that has won some awards is different yet again. Picking one is like picking a favorite child.

That said, the best book for your customer might not be any of the ones I already mentioned, and discerning that can sometimes be guesswork, but it's made easier if you've identified your audience.

I use a little rule of thumb for what I am pitching: if their eye is visibly drawn to one book's cover or if they pick up a book, *that* is the book I'm going all in on pitching. This is partly why it's so important to have covers that are highly professional, very appealing, and on point for their genre.

Another rule of thumb is that you don't want to overload people. I have a couple versions of my pitches, as I've already mentioned. If I have sussed out that I'll need to give an overview pitch of multiple books. (That's usually when someone tells me they read "everything.") I'll give the shortened versions until I see his or her eyebrows arch, or some other sign that they are intrigued. Then I'll launch into a slightly deeper pitch in my attempt to hook them as a reader.

4. Try to sell more than one at a time. I mean two things by this. First, I mean go for the upsell. If you have a series, try to sell the whole series. You can incentivize it in a few ways. The only time I give discounts are on multi-book bundles. Sometimes I do an additional giveaway with a nice screen-printed fabric bag to carry multiple books.

I'll talk some more about pricing in the next chapter, but the only time I use price as an incentive is when it increases the total profit. I sell value rather than discount myself. You will never, ever, be able to out-discount the big publishing houses because of the bulk printing rates that they can get by printing tens of thousands of copies at a time. They also have a marketing and distribution presence that creates organic reach that you won't be able to touch. But you have something those publishers do not have: *you*. They don't have what you're selling, and you'll be able to leverage buyers with tactics that the big publishers can't—and *that's* where you live. The big publishers access their own toolbox. Don't play a game that is rigged in their favor when you have your own set of tools that they only wish they could tap into. We'll discuss the math of it all later.

There is another way I up my sales. I use a loud voice when I pitch a book (part of that is my natural enthusiasm, and now it's become second nature.) I'm always pitching my book to the guy behind whomever is at my table as well. People regularly overhear something in a book pitch that makes them stop and listen. It is very often the second person at the table who actually buys your book ... and that leads me to the next point.

5. Nothing draws a crowd like a crowd. In my 20 years of nonprofit work with teenagers, I noticed a difference in mindsets between age brackets. Younger teens/Junior high students ask, "What are we doing?" Older teens and young adults ask, "Who is going to be there?" I'm convinced this is tied to our psychological need to be involved in community. I've seen sitcoms that play with this notion, too, with curious people just stepping into a long line that wraps around a building. They don't necessarily know what the line is for, but people seem excited and eager for it, whatever it is, and so the characters get in line. Hilarity ensues.

It's the same way at events. If one or two people stop to talk or browse, more will do so, too. People are interested *because other people are interested*. That is partly why I learned to pitch everyone, but then zero in on the person who is ready to move to the POS. This functions about the same as shifting *what* I'm pitching to whatever book someone gravitates towards most. Harness enthusiasm and move them to the POS.

Sometimes at a show, I'll have family or friends show up as booth helpers. They will inevitably stretch their legs and do a walk around the show and then stop in front of the table for a quick chat. Occasionally, friendly vendors who I know from other shows will do the same. The other vendors (if they've been doing shows for any length of time,) know that the purpose of my presence is to make sales. If a customer comes up and starts looking, the conversation usually ends with a friendly nod and wave implying we can pick up the chat again later … they were useful *and they* helped draw in a customer because a crowd creates a crowd.

6. Ditch your family. Well, *not really*, but you should be brutally honest with your family and friends to help set expectations before the show starts. Conventions and large events can be a lot of fun, but you are also there to work, and as the boss and also the primary driving workforce of your booth and sales efforts, you've got to do some actual work. I was running a booth for a traditional publisher and watched a booth-mate who did not understand this. As a young author, also signed to that publisher, he had his first book out, and we were pitching it at this literary festival. His father came to "just hang out" and keep his young adult son company.

The son was a little socially awkward, and so I believe the father thought he was helping. He was not. If he was helping pitch the book, he could have been a tremendous help, but he was having long drawn-out conversations with his son instead, enough that the son could not engage any potential readers. He had very few interactions or sales because of it.

Your family and close friends can be either a distraction or a boon. Make sure you set some clear expectations, or you'll be constantly finding errands to send them on, as I did with this father. Just to free up a window to have conversations with potential buyers, I sent him to fetch water bottles, check on various things, and whatnot.

Conversations and having fun with friends and family is highly encouraged! But make sure that they know where your focus is. This is hard to learn, and it chaffed some feelings when I first set boundaries early on, but I have a great system (which most vendors intuitively understand - a conversation might end mid-sentence even, and resume again thirty minutes later in the exact same place once the space has cleared and a lull in traffic develops.

7. Have a secondary objective. I do this a lot while I am working the buttons on the transaction in my POS. There are several seconds of lag time in which you can make a secondary pitch. This could be a last-second Hail Mary to add on a second book, or work in an upsell/bundle if that applies. It's also a great spot to try to insert someone onto your newsletter list by offering a free ebook.

I mostly do comic book conventions and so my nerdy murder mystery at comic-con is my best-selling book. I know how keenly targeted my audience is for this show and that the back cover hook sells the book so well I don't have to put much effort into it. If a customer is buying any other book and hasn't looked at 50 Shades of Worf, I hand over a copy and say, "While I'm ringing you up, just read the back cover." That usually results in snorts of laughter and very often becomes an add on to the sale. You can only do this if your target is laser focused, and the blurb is tight, snappy, and flows smoothly (mine is also very short). If you can pull this off, you can dramatically increase your sales at the POS. It's like getting super-sized without the heart attacks.

8. Smile—even if it's fake. I've said it before, drink if you have to. It's still a joke, kind of. It actually comes from a possible Hemingway quote, "Write drunk, edit sober." There's a reason I listed ibuprofen on the supply list. You will need to do everything you can to remain relatively comfortable. Connecting with people is imperative. Smiling is huge, and sincerity goes a long way … if you can't be sincere when you smile, try fake smiling. A phony smile is still better than no smile.

9. Have more than one book. I speak to a lot of authors and would-be-authors at events, and I have a couple pieces of advice that never change. One is to give explicit permission to one or two people to be honestly critical about your book so you can refine it before publication. (Ideally, it's someone who doesn't like you all that much—and then just ignore anything intentionally spiteful.) The

second is to write short fiction. Just today, I gave homework to a young writer with her novel manuscript that is about to wrap up writing this week. "Write five different short stories of 10,000 words, and then write another five of 1,000 … the latter will be the hardest." This not only helps refine the writing craft, but it also teaches how to edit and revise a story to completion without each draft taking months or weeks. After my first couple of novels were completed, I wrote short fiction exclusively for about two years and it dramatically improved my storytelling.

There is a secondary reason, too. You can submit these stories to anthology collections, and you can usually buy these collections at cost and sell them at your table as well. This gives you more product to catch eyes and appeal to buyers by having a slightly broader range of items. You can also compile your collected and edited short stories into a personal anthology for an additional book.

This is a relatively easy way to get some additional products on your table and then open up bundling options in addition to making you a better writer by helping improve your craft. These short stories can also function as reader magnets, which I already mentioned when discussing newsletter sign-ups and Newsletter Ninja. You can also build a small backlist by releasing them as ebook versions.

10. Get Rest. Some shows will offer a special block rate for vendors and attendees at hotels. This is more likely to happen in downtown locations where hotels might be more difficult to get last minute or if the hotels are sponsor partners of the event. I rarely stay in these for two reasons. First, they are usually much more expensive than other options. Also, while convenient and close, and though they sometimes offset any parking fees, that is not always the case. The convenience of proximity is usually not worth the added cost. I usually stay at the convention block if it's a show I'm doing more for fun than for profit. This is typically the case if I'm on vacation or bringing family. The second reason is that

conventions bring out the fun side in everybody, even ardent wallflowers. That sounds great—but it means you run the risk of loud people in the hallways keeping you from sleep. Smaller options like B&Bs are great because you know the rest will be great and you won't be disturbed by a partying college lacrosse team.

If you want to get actual rest so you can perform best and also save a few bucks on lodging, look for clean and convenient options ten to fifteen miles away. I've stayed in some pretty sketchy places to save money. In my mind, I'm here for the con, not the after events ... except for certain shows where I plan for some evening fun so it's okay to plan for a little fun. Just remember that cutting costs is a surefire way to improve your bottom line.

In my earlier days, I would often find other folks doing the same events to split hotel and travel costs with. I still do that on occasion, and it is a great solution to steep entry costs. Other options are OTAs like Airbnb, traditional bed and breakfasts, and things like Couchsurfer, or even camping. At some large shows, I've rented entire houses and then found other vendors to take the individual rooms for a portion of the cost, leveraging the effort of a group and resulting in drastically lower costs.

11. Avoid Booth Barnacles. You know barnacles ... they're those nuisance crustaceans that attach themselves to ships and won't let go. They hamper a ship by slowing it down, increasing resistance, and creating drag that kills fuel economy in newer ships. In the Golden Age of Piracy, crafts that needed speed would actually beach themselves to remove barnacles which slowed their ships.

At any show with vendors, you will have rows and rows of people who paid good money to be present; these people are effectively stuck at their booths. Some folks (and this often includes the socially awkward who haven't learned social cues), have learned that vendors can't escape. Beware the socially awkward extrovert. Once they realize that they literally have a captive audience, things can become difficult.

I don't think that there is anything particularly nefarious about *most* booth barnacles, and I've made friends and even repeat customers with some of them who I see often, but it is helpful to have a barnacle mitigation plan. As a general rule of thumb, these are not buyers. True booth barnacles are there to have conversations and interactions and have no interest in your book (or usually any product outside a narrow band of fandom which drew them to the event in the first place.) Those who are merely socially awkward can still be sold to, though it may take some additional finesse and time to bring them to the POS. Those who are merely slower on social convention may still hang around a little, and that is okay (nothing draws a crowd like a crowd), but true barnacles try to make the whole engagement about whatever motive *they* have in mind and will steer away from your pitch and products in an attempt to control the engagement. While they can be handy at being part of a crowd, aggressive barnacles can sometimes alienate/chase away actual buyers like a baby cuckoo kicking eggs out of the nest.

If I believe I've become infested with a booth barnacle, my go-to maneuver is to change into a hard sell. That is sometimes enough to dislodge it. It may take some time and feel heartless, because it's hard to tell the difference between a booth barnacle and someone who might be socially delayed. It's a gut call that you'll have to make, and it's something you'll have to learn by doing—this has to be more caught than taught.

I also know that of all the things I've written, this is the one most likely to earn me some hate mail. *I don't care*. I stand by what I've said: there are some people who have ulterior motives in this world, and they sometimes disguise themselves as socially awkward or hide behind similar traits. (Lord knows that often describes *me, too*). If you don't want your business to suffer, you must learn to navigate that murky water, and you will probably make a wrong call sometimes. But you are running a business, not a charity or outreach. I'm not saying to be heartless, but I am advocating wisdom and giving you permission to scrape off the barnacles when you have cause... you'll go faster, and you'll sail further.

The presence of booth barnacles is true at all types of expos, though they may be more prevalent at comic book conventions which, by the nature of their fandoms' history, have catered to the awkward and disenfranchised (also part of why I enjoy them). If you have booth helpers, you can often disengage by letting them run interference for you.

But disengaging is not always as easy as merely shrugging and saying, "Well, enjoy the rest of the show." I have a backup move that I've had to employ at times. "I really have to use the restroom, so I have to leave." But booth barnacles are sticky things. I had one braggart who kept trying to tell me stories about his doubtful past accomplishments, Uncle Rico style, even after a hard sell and the admission that he had no intention of buying anything.

Barnacle: "Hey have you heard about XYZ?"

Me: "No. And I'm sorry, but I've really got to focus on customers. I'm here to sell books."

Barnacle: "Oh, that's okay. I'll tell you anyway."

Me: visible confusion.

My wife, behind me: not-so-subtle laughter.

Certain he would've just followed me if I headed towards the restroom, I started pitching someone else, even though they were further away and had not established eye contact. They did come over and listen to me pitching each book while the barnacle stood there, searching for an opening to steer the conversation back to him and his stories. I ignored him, but it took several minutes before the barnacle eventually departed. My saviors also had no intention of buying but understood that something was awry based on the look in my eyes. It was kind of like pretending to be some random female stranger's boyfriend for two minutes to scare off an unwanted male follower.

Speaking of that, there are a few booth barnacle subspecies for whom I have no tolerance. It is okay to have a violent reaction against them (usually involving yelling, pointing, and warning other vendors/event organizers about them.)

One is the predator/pervert. Yes, there may be folks with downright rapey intentions at large events. Conventions are not unlike *everywhere else* in the world, and this is always a problem, so have a plan to deal with it and know where safe spaces/people are located. I think I give off a protective dad vibe (probably because my daughter often does events with me). I've had younger girls sometimes hang out near me at events and later tell me it's because of a local stalker they'd picked up and I looked scary enough to deter them. Another kind are stolen valor bros. These are folks who will go beyond merely embellishing military records, but will outright make up stories, always to make themselves out to be heroes/bad-ass Rambo types. You never hear one brag about working in a motor pool or their clerical duties—they've always got stories about being a member of special forces or sent on covert operations. I was talking about guns with a sword and weapons vendor I know when one such barnacle came up. He got many details about military weapons very, very wrong.

Another vendor and actual veteran came up after and said, "I saw you talking to that guy ... he's full of shit and if he tries to talk to me again, he'll be lucky to leave with his teeth." That veteran had actually been in a conflict the barnacle was bragging about, though replete with inaccuracies.

The last type is those trying to sell me something. These are the least likely to be socially awkward or potentially suffering from some sort of mental defect. You could make the argument that these barnacles are the most calculating type. They're on the hunt for new agents in their Multi-Level Marketing plan (pyramid scheme,) signing people up for a cult, or some other such venture. These barnacles are actively and knowingly stealing from you by taking your time away from your booth (which you've paid money to have a presence). Time spent listening to a grifter is time you can't use to sell.

You'll find your own way around the barnacles, and you won't always encounter them at shows, but know that they are out there, and be prepared to deal with them if necessary … and most of all, don't let them stop you from selling your book.

12. Have help. Whenever possible, bring a friend. Sometimes you need an extra runner to grab coffee for you or get something from your car. A helper could help keep you alert if they made the trip for you and they'll keep you awake (hopefully) on late drives. Most importantly, they can help you make sales by helping pitch during very busy times, or even just running the POS if they are introverts. Even incremental help can let you maximize your pitching potential.

13. Go into a show with goals. Having a finish line to shoot for is a good idea. It will push you to keep pitching, even if you get tired or your attitude wavers. It may seem like an arbitrary number, since *you* made the goal, but it helps win the psychological war. This number is not the same as your break-even number. If you've been at this a while, it should be higher than a 0-baseline. When I was first starting out, mine wasn't even at the break-even line … it was just to recoup table expenses. But you'll have to start somewhere and then scale up by making the right moves and building the right habits.

Presently, I set two goals: 1) what I think the show should realistically be able to offer me in terms of sales based on research, past experience with the event/chain/area, etc. and 2) how many sales I *want* to do (keep it a realistic number).

Knowing your shows' general flow is also very helpful. You can't look at your current sales number and simply multiply them by the hours in your show, etc. At most cons I do I know that my busiest traffic flow is 11:30-1:30, then it tapers down for a few hours, then spikes, falls off again, and then there is a slight uptick shortly before close. Most of those are very serious buyers because they are racing a clock to make purchases. Your POS can track when sales are made and provide further insight into your peak sales times and days as well. It's good to review that data.

I talk with a lot of vendors. Most of them completely disregard Sunday because it feels slower. However, I often sell best on the last day and have many folks I pitched earlier in the show return to buy on Sunday. Trends will also shift, too, so don't put too much stock in them. Pre-COVID, my Fridays were roughly 80% as good as my Saturday sales. But once shows returned after lockdown, the Tier 2 events I did were posting abysmal numbers on Fridays. I pitched and pitched and pitched and people were very interested, but would ultimately say, "Thank you," and walk away. But many of them came back on Saturday and Sunday and bought later, so you can't compare trends from previous times or shows to the one you're at now. Every show is its own unique animal. When I looked at those Tier 2 shows, sales overall were okay, even if the Friday numbers were so low I wanted to up and leave the convention. (I never worked so hard in my life to sell a mere 9-15 books ... but like a rubber band, I'd sell 80-120 on each of the next two days.)

14. Don't get distracted with swag. Or with other things. Even costuming, panels and workshops, and other aspects of a convention can get in the way of your main goal: selling more books. Remember to *keep the main thing the main thing.*

I see lots of authors try to fill out their table by making t-shirts, and book bags, and posters, and bracelets, and a million other things. Don't go broke trying to make swag. I fell into this trap early on, too, and then I realized what I wrote previously: nobody is coming to the event looking for you. (With family being the exception.)

Similarly, nobody is buying and wearing your swag except your mom. I have seen a lot of authors try to diversify their table, but branded swag just doesn't sell. To wear a t-shirt or have an appreciation for the stuff, a customer must already be a super-fan and have your book ... meaning the best secondary item to sell is *another book.*

Most branded swag is so unprofitable that it doesn't make sense, but authors tend to justify it as "marketing," or what not, but even DIY stuff takes such a larger investment of time that it doesn't make financial sense. Even selling your hand-knit earmuffs or home-baked cookie widgets distracts from your main thing. If you get a big following on your hand-crafted dragon finger puppets, you'll wind up spending your time with felt and glue guns instead of at the keyboard building your next book. Authoring is a long-term industry, and swag can create a distraction if you let it. I'm not saying don't ever do it, *but I am saying* you risk making a ton of waste by taking your eyes off the goal.

15. Manage your booth space. I mentioned visibility before and just discussed swag. One problem with swag is the tendency to overload your booth with non-bookish things or to obscure what your table is about. Just like a good book cover communicates the genre of your book, a good table, at a glance, tells your audience what you are selling and what kind of books you write.

Regularly revisit your appearance. Try different layouts and arrangements. Face out and give attention to what book is your biggest seller. And if it becomes necessary, pay for larger or premium space—that should be part of your plan to scale up. I know that's where I am. I need to get multiple tables when it is possible, but it is not always something I can do due to space concerns, especially at larger shows.

16. Focus your energy on the most productive elements. This is a suggestion that can be applied to more than just your book sales. Regarding the live event sales, having at least a year's worth of data will bring clarity to where you are succeeding, and therefore where you should increase your attention to bring better profits.

For example, I write a couple of different series and I have to decide which book I will write during which season. If a particular series has been showing a considerable amount of popularity versus the other ones, I will work on writing a new book on that series next. The new book should continue to drive more sales and breathe more life into it, giving the series a kind of snowball effect.

Sometimes the refocus is due to a more short-term situation; you may have to pivot and refocus on the fly. I was at a 70,000 attendee convention that was very busy (it had shorter vendor hall hours than I was used to, but I was doing at least $1,000 per day for each of the show's 4 days.) With that many people, inconvenient infrastructure snafus popped up. Namely, related to the Wi-Fi. I couldn't get a consistent enough signal to connect to my POS. I was able to engineer a workaround on the fly with my backup, but spending time trying to get my newsletter sign-up device up and running would have cost me hundreds of dollars in sales.

Pivot. Refocus.

I concentrated instead on telling folks about what kind of content they'd get by being on my newsletter and pointing them to resources on my website and the scan-able QR code on my backdrop materials. Knowing that this particular show was extremely loud due to the sheer volume of bodies in the convention center, building a deeper rapport with browsers was difficult and costly (there is a danger in losing one's voice) meaning I went into it focused on direct sales. NL sign-ups and immediate onboarding had to take a backseat. In this case, I pivoted away from almost entirely unless buyers asked for directly.

I want to repeat the number one thing you must do at your booth: ask for the sale. Once moving to the POS, go for the upsell! The number one way to increase your sales and profits is to increase the number of items sold by add-ons, book bundles, omnibuses, etc. To do that, create value without taking significant hits on your profit margins.

Chapter Ten:
In the Booth Part 3
(Little Cautionary Tales)

There are a few other things worth knowing about selling at live events, and so I'll talk about them here. These are pieces of advice that don't really fit into any specific category, and some of these you will have no control over, but knowledge is power and simply being aware of certain kinds of situations may come in handy. Forewarned is forearmed. These are all little cautionary tales that you might glean some insight from, so I share them here for your education and amusement.

Booth Placement

Traffic might not always flow the way you'd expect. For *most* shows, I don't get an option for placement or location, but will be able to book a *type* of location. Artist tables are generally cheaper but often smaller; booths generally have better locations in the way of traffic and closer to entry points. Both varieties often have premium locations that may be end-caps, corners, or have special placement. Traffic patterns can create very weird dynamics and sometimes have contrary expectations. I'll post a few stories to demonstrate.

"The chute." I shared a table with a fellow author at a decent show I've done several times. The show was small so we had to keep spaces tight, but it was only a couple years into my doing lots of conventions and I was only just beginning to scale up. We had an opportunity to take the first booth directly at the mouth of the con's entrance. There was literally no way to walk past either of us without passing our booth. We were pretty excited.

We posted terrible numbers, and this was a show that we both typically did very well at. Instead of selling lots of books over three days, we did lots of people watching and I learned to follow people's eyes. They looked right past us as if we'd become invisible.

The audience was in a hurry to get in and didn't pay attention to their surroundings until they were twenty feet inside the event, so 2-3 booths deep. I've watched this phenomenon occur at other places too and it has bitten me in the rear a few times (that bad Barnes and Noble show I mentioned earlier was a direct result of this, only it was even more out of sight than in "the chute"). Sometimes, now that I've taken a keen interest in this, I watch for it at other places and see it play out at other events and places where I am shopping.

"Shademongers." I picked my spot at a renfest where approved weekend vendors got to set up tents. I've attended this show previously (as both vendor and attendee,) so I knew it well. There was one tree in the area, and it always got hot around midday so I set up where I knew the shade would be around that time. I felt so clever at having such foresight.

Nearby, around 1 pm, there was a gypsy belly dancing class and some other activities which drew a crowd. That's all well and good, but afterward, they moved and a crew of about 45 came and plopped down in the shade, encamping around me. I watched my wonderfully engineered traffic pattern shift because people had to walk around the crowd that sat lounging. They kept in the shade for almost an hour before things finally reverted to normal, and for that entire time, I could not even make eye contact with potential buyers. They'd taken a new route that was far out of my proximity.

I must have looked irked, because the person in charge realized later what was going on and apologized when the group finally moved off. This kind of clumping has happened to me again at conventions during autograph signing times when posted too close to celebrities and lines can sometimes grow to block traffic. I always imagined those in line would be a kind of captive audience to show books to—but they really are not. Those in line for something else don't typically have the bandwidth for one more new thing (especially something that moves them out of the line they are in).

"Tough corners." Just like in the earlier chute, where people are moving quickly and blindly to get past a choke point, some corners can be like this, especially inside corners facing outside walls.

I've paid an obscene amount of money at shows to test different foot traffic dynamics. At one of these, I opted to upgrade into a premium corner booth. My placement was near the door and on the edge, near the outside wall. People look beyond the part they walk around, only watching it in their peripheral vision. Because they have to hug the inside of the lane, they walk faster and "look past" what is there, reducing your visibility and ability to engage. I've watched it happen a lot with traffic flow patterns at places like Sam's Club and Costco where certain corners can make the free-sample slingers placed there look cloaked like a Klingon bird of prey ... even free mini-weenies have a hard time putting them on peoples' radar.

But I did get some data at that show and another author who has similar success and uses long-honed sales tactics was also at that show. She had two tables purchased in the author alley (which had pretty decent placement, in fact) and she did roughly 90% of what I did in sales numbers ... but for half the cost of a "premium booth."

Artist vs. Vendor spots

I am generally of the opinion that people are more prepared to make purchases in the vendor section than in the artist alley area. For artists, some folks are more inclined to only browse. Depending on the show, that may be the case and I used to pay the extra money in order to be in the vendor area, as opposed to the author/artist area.

I've come to the opposite conclusion after many years. Shoppers in the vendor section are typically looking for collectibles and items already licensed in their favorite fandoms and shoppers in the artist area are often searching specifically for indie creators.

Earlier, I mentioned that artist alley tables are often cheaper than full booths. They typically run 25-50% of the standard booth cost, at least at events I go to. I have seen that some craft bazaars and maker shows have reduced rates for people who create their own products versus resellers of products like Tupperware, Lululemon, Mary Kay, etc. but not all do. It may be worth asking about an artist or maker rate when you are purchasing space. There are some smaller shows that I have done previously, and I really want to support the show, but without an artist rate it becomes impossible for me to post a profit and so I quit their shows and explained why. Sometimes promoters need to hear that kind of feedback.

For artist space, I spend on average about $350 for a Tier 1 show, $200-250 at a Tier 2, $100-150 for a Tier 3 show, and $100-125 for a Tier 4. Because those smaller shows are often in less busy/saturated places, finding quality lodging for lower prices is often easier which offsets costs even though there is not a significant drop-off in cost of entry.

Whichever space you choose, be sure you read the show's rules and regulations. It's worth knowing which ones you can bend a little and which rules are firm. This is going to vary and could also change at the drop of a dime, and with the whims and moods of volunteers. Many of them let power go to their heads and they will take their role far more seriously than Paul Blart, Mall Cop, ever did.

At one show, a Karen cut through my corner booth—literally walked behind my table and crossed through my vendor space—as a shortcut. My back was turned for a moment and I turned back in full Wolverine cosplay; she gasped and recoiled when she saw my prop claws and then booked it away. Whatever motivated her hurried shortcut through my booth didn't prevent a detour for her to complain to security that "some crazed vendor nearly stabbed me with wolverine claws." I got a stern talking to by volunteer security who seemed to think I'd hidden a bomb in a hockey puck somewhere (that's a Threat Level Midnight reference). I explained what had happened, but Paul Blart Junior stood watch for a while and kept trying to give me orders until he called his supervisor, who was on con staff. She listened to the volunteer's beef with me, rolled her eyes at the security guy, and said, "Really? You called me down for this?" I had to deal with dirty looks whenever he passed later, but the trouble ended. Just remember, if you play fast and loose with the rules, the show is within their rights to kick you out. It's rare, but I *have* seen it before, and I *have* seen con staff go as far as measuring display heights on backdrops, etc. and forcing vendors to lower them.

Food Vendors

I am glad that many shows have a variety of food options. Some shows create a kind of food court area—but I *hate* being posted near the food court.

The food court creates a few problems, and all of them are distractions. During feeding times, there is an influx of people to the area, but they are moving with speed and purpose and so you have "the chute" problems compounded by the same problems of "the shademongers" as the lines develop. People won't step out of line if you pitch them because they are obeying their stomachs.

Couple those issues with the smells of food and the fear of the commissary running low on nuggies or funnel cakes and things get difficult within a certain proximity. Nearby placement doesn't make it impossible, but things don't go nearly as smoothly. Also, you get food comas and the recently fed tend to lay lethargic, sunning themselves after gorging upon fried nourishment as they wait to shed their skin due to the size increase. (I know you think I'm talking about snakes, but it also applies to cosplayers.)

Another reason I hate being located near the food court is a practical one. They are just so incredibly loud. You wouldn't think it possible, but it is one of the noisiest places. Without booths and other vendors nearby to absorb the sound, the volume can get dreadfully high, which brings us to another issue: raw noise.

Volume

I admit to having a voice that travels, but even I can't compete with the noise of large and loud conventions. Tier 1 and 2 shows are usually in big arenas with high ceilings and there's very little to mitigate noise. Between the constant use of your voice for pitching and the projection required to be heard, this can prove to be an obstacle. I bring lots of fluids to keep my throat from drying up.

Losing your voice is a very real concern, especially in the Tier 1 shows which cost the most. If your voice gives out on you, your booth is practically dead in the water. I bring drinks in during my setup and leave them hidden in my booth because some shows don't allow outside food or drink. I don't drink beverages with sugar in them and onsite vendors (who will gladly sell you a $6 can of soda) don't usually have sugar-free options because who needs to live past fifty, anyway? Vendors usually get some leeway on this rule, but it's easier if you bring in those supplies at the beginning than worry about it later when your voice begins to crack.

I'd like to take a moment to issue a public service announcement...

People who play music as part of their cosplay are allowed to be hit by cars. This is my pet peeve and this is my book, so I'm not going to pull any punches ... this is the modern equivalent to those 80s metal punks with boom boxes who walked around forcing everyone to listen to their music while being a general jack-wagon to their neighbors. Remember when Spock knocked out that guy in the fourth motion picture? That's my chief temptation at conventions.

On a more serious note, though, some costumers *insist* on cranking loud music as part of their shtick and they generally feel obligated to max out the volume knob and then break it off so nobody can turn it down. The real reason is less malicious. Conventions are loud and they can't hear their own music so they turn it way up, not realizing they're contributing to the problem.

When you're trying to make a connection and close a sale, and one of those guys interrupts or drowns out your voice, it can be frustrating. Most shows have rules against it, but they are seldom enforced ... though it is more likely that a *booth* running music or loud audio will be asked to shut it down since they are easier to police. Playing music during setup is usually fine, but when the crowd noise is in full swing, pumping up your volume so you can hear your tunes makes you a bad booth neighbor.

What happens when the problem is the *convention?* It can happen. I did a show where the promoter let his nephew, an aspiring singer/songwriter, have the stage where he overwhelmed the show with volume as he murdered a bunch of cover tunes with malice (though his original stuff was actually decent). After enough folks asked, con staff brought the volume down to a reasonable level because people had begun avoiding the vendor hall because of it. In subsequent years, they made sure not to make the same mistake. Conventions work a lot like the way America's political system is *supposed* to work. If there is enough support for or against something, change will happen. Big shows are businesses at their core, and they know if they alienate their vendors/patrons, they won't return. No vendors = no show since they rely on booked space to secure deposits early in the planning stages.

Loudspeaker announcements can also be an interruption, but are usually infrequent. One of my favorite shows runs regular announcements and recently had a very good announcer for their entertainment hall. He would do an announcement every 1-2 hours through the show to promote things, give reminders, etc. Then it came very frequently—and the volume was such that you could not talk over it. It became annoying after regular interruptions, but I'd had enough after no fewer than six interruptions while I was still with the same customer (not an exaggeration, and it may have been closer to 10). He really was clever and a good MC—but he was frustrating my customer interactions and so I sent a simple message to the con staff after asking my booth neighbors if they were annoyed by it too. "Dealing with a lot of noise problems in Artist Alley. Can we ask that you keep non-emergency announcements to only once every 30-60 minutes? The interruptions are impacting convos with customers." Got a prompt apology, and they scaled it back … the announcer had gone a little rogue with the microphone.

Know who on con staff can help with issues, but don't abuse them. It's worth asking others first to check if it's just a poor attitude on your part or if there's an actual concern. Sometimes you're just hangry and need a Snickers. Sometimes, concerns really do need to be addressed.

A solid cover

Oftentimes, a book cover is the last thing most authors think about, but the first thing that buyers see. It is also your single greatest marketing tool, so put a sexy car body around that big and fast engine you just built. I know that this shouldn't have to be said … but it does. It really, really does, because in the dozens of shows I attend every year, I see the same mistakes regarding covers. And there are a lot of authors who don't understand why their books aren't selling.

Quite honestly, I know *this* book will sell well because I understand how buyers arrive at a purchasing decision and how the cover relates to that process. I sell something like 10-20 times more books than most authors I meet at events. Those gains would likely be cut in half or more simply by having a good cover. It is a difficult thing to tell an author, "Your cover is awful and it is the reason why your book is not selling well." It's up there with, "How did your baby get so ugly?"

Earlier in this book, I stressed the importance of giving someone explicit permission to be critical with your manuscript. Do this with your covers, too. (Ideally *before* you release them.) I redid the covers on my sci-fi series and immediately had a 600% increase in sales. One of them had a sub-par cover, the other was great but not on brand for the genre, and so it created resistance to purchasing.

A word of warning: not every artist should be designing covers. That does not mean they are bad artists, but cover design is a different skill entirely and cover elements are not the same as with other art.

Another warning: don't let your child, friend, or spouse make your cover for you! At the last show I did, I heard three authors on different occasions talk about how they'd saved money by having their "very talented teenage artist" do their cover. (We authors do love to talk and share our process.) Saving money is great, but your cover is not as much an expense as it is *an investment*.

Consider this: what if the book's sales are performing poorly? Maybe the art is phenomenal, but it doesn't make for a good cover. A good piece of art does not necessarily equate to a good cover. If you use a loved one's cover and it performs badly, you can't likely change the cover. *Ever.* You're locked into using it at the risk of hurting their feelings. And if it continues to do badly (and it will) you're subjecting them to negativity—remember that you will hear a lot of unbidden critical feedback in the form of online reviews or directly from potential customers. I consulted with one author via my blog, and I explained that the sticking point was his covers, done by his teenage child, and he understood that he could never change it. The only conclusion we could arrive at was that he had to throw away his entire 5-book fantasy series and do something completely new and different. It was the only path forward for him since he'd committed to never altering his cover and making it marketable. That's a lot of hours spent behind a keyboard now gone to waste.

There are lots of online groups devoted to helping you get a high-quality cover for a decent price, or reviewing what you have and providing constructive feedback before you're hit by internet trolls. Use those resources and you'll be money ahead!

Chapter Eleven: Magic Bullets

There is no real "magic bullet," or "One Insane Trick to Force Readers to Buy Your Book." Headlines like that are all trying to sell you something, and that something doesn't exist. I'm sure you've seen a plethora of articles with headlines like that. Most of them were paid or sponsored posts (read: Ads) meant to make you click in the hope of either selling something or generating affiliate cash.

That's partly how you know my book's content is legit. I'm telling you the opposite of what you want to hear. There is no trick to this: *it's all work*. But as my father always told me, "Work smarter, not harder ... well, work harder *and* smarter." Equipped with knowledge and a little guidance, you *can* achieve your goal ... selling more books at live events.

Instead of magic bullets and new weird tricks, find your method. Research your niche and put in the preparation work. Once you find what works for you, try tweaking and altering that by degrees to optimize your success and build on it. I see many people in all disciplines chasing someone *else's* success. Don't abandon moderate success because someone else is doing well with something different. Here's an example: I see authors abandoning their newsletters and other tried-and-true tactics to jump on things like TikTok and other new and trendy platforms. If those are good services for you, by all means explore them, but don't burn down something you've begun to build on your way out the door. Everything is new at some point, but wade in as you find success. Don't pull out of something that works reasonably well for you because another person has wild success elsewhere and bank on that being your million-dollar magic bullet. It won't be.

Wade in. Scale up.

That said, don't run out and buy tables for every Tier 1 show you can find and buy 3,000 copy print runs on all your books to sell. You'll go broke housing your stock. Start somewhere that you feel capable and then build off what works. Probably don't even make a run at a Tier 1 show in your first year unless you are splitting costs with another author/artist and you just want a comparative experience as you build your live sales experience.

The Competition

I wrote much earlier that you shouldn't feel threatened or in direct competition with other authors. Not only do we love to talk and share about what works for us (at least that is the case for most of us who last beyond their first few live events or book releases), but we all have our own vibe and unique approach to selling. When you do shows, it may be advantageous to keep a notebook and write down the things you see that others are using to their advantage.

Through conversations and directly asking what seems to be working for others, you might be turned on to new ideas or tactics. Before implementing them, you might try searching the internet for more information. The tactic might be something from which you can glean even greater insight on by searching online ... or maybe you'll do some research and realize that it's actually a terrible idea for some reason or another and the excited vendor happens to be caught in a stroke of luck which is sure to run out.

Remember, nobody else has your particular book. *They need what you offer.* Sell browsers on *that.* Don't try to price match other authors. (I share several real examples of this principle in action inside the free, bonus chapter on pricing.)

A lot of folks I personally know do the convention special pricing or will round down to the nearest increment of 5 because $15 for a book is convenient. I've done the math and the statistics and know that I'd be losing a couple thousand dollars per year if I did that. How great would it be to get a $2,000 annual raise over last year's wages? It's nothing to sniff at, and it also helps keep you on the level with your tax obligations.

Here's my advice in a nutshell. Don't let your competitors dictate what you are going to do. They're not selling your book and so they don't have any say. I was just at a show where another competitor was selling books in the same genre as me (albeit with subpar covers, but with a higher quality printer—she used Ingramspark while I carry 80% of my stock from the cheaper alternative). I outsold her by huge magnitudes—and that's with her convention pricing of $13 per book. I looked her dead in the eyes and told her, "You're undercharging for your books." And then I told her why (even though my wife insists I need to stop giving away free advice and start charging for my consults.) I am confident that this other author would have tripled her sales by following the advice I've laid out here and it would not have reduced my sales one bit.

The Gameplan

Hopefully, you've got the idea that you ought to prepare a plan of attack for your live sales events. I advise you to write down as much as you can—at least the basic details. Not only will it reinforce how you should plan and sell, but it will also reinforce in your mind exactly what you are going to do. The better you know the plan, the more likely you are to execute it with quality and diligence.

You will need to scale up and into your game plan, but your plan going in should include this:

- Engage potential buyers
- Sell more books by upselling and averaging a sale of 1.5 books per transaction or better
- Onboard as many new people as possible to your Newsletter
- Use omnibus editions to increase your profit margins. (I count every three-book omnibus sold as three books for tracking purposes.)
- Only offer deals on packages/bundles that encourage binging
- Sell value and show what the buyer is getting instead of pushing the idea of savings
- Keep production costs low, but quality, and search for expenses that can be reduced
- Track as much as you can so you can best determine what kind of shows are most profitable for you
- Manage your stock well (selling out = losing potential sales)
- Maintain your attitude and stay excited about your books! If your book doesn't excite you, pull back, hire an editor or whatever you need to do to improve and make it *good*. As Pam once said on The Office, "Please don't throw garbage at me." Don't throw it at your customers, either.

The Girl Scout Paradox

Waaaaay back in the Intro, I encouraged you to look at the Girl Scouts and their cookie selling mafia. I've repeatedly said, "Nobody else has what you are selling." But what about when that's not quite true?

Very often writers one table away are selling the same genre, and sometimes even pitching it the same way. How can I not feel like we are competing for the same buyers?

I spent three days talking to a kid, the son of another vendor, who really loved fantasy. He actually went to a friend of mine (another high fantasy author) and bought that guy's books instead of mine. I honestly didn't feel bad about it. I was happy for my friend and the fact that this teenager was reading. I know, I'm a saint and my optimism is a testament to my kind. (Actually, I have a rule that I never expect vendors or their kids to buy my stuff—despite the fact that they often do... I just think it's unfair to expect other people hustling for sales to be out shopping.)

But here's my thing about the Girl Scouts: the exact same cookies that they're selling outside my local WalMart are available *inside* the store and on the shelf. At least the good ones are. They've got knock off thin mints, peanut butter whatchamawhoozits, coconut thingies, and more inside the WalMart cookie aisle ... and for a fraction or the cost. I feel like I was freakin red pilled by Morpheus. "What if I told you they have Thin Mints for a dollar fifty?"

Sometimes a product might be similar. A lot of things are. That's why we use "High Concept" pitches: to harness the appeal of the familiar. (An example I used earlier was my Shadowless pitch. "Imagine I Am Legend occurs in a world like City of Ember." They might know both, or maybe only one of the references, but either is likely to trigger a positive response in my target audience.)

When things are similar, *sell yourself.*

Remember that *you* are what makes your product unique. If you connect with a potential reader at a relationship level, that will be what earns you the sale—and if not now, then it will likely materialize later. And get that person onto your mailing list! If they like you, they'll want to hear more from you—and not just every now and then when you happen to push out a new book in their preferred genre.

The Girl Scouts: we could learn a lot from them. I'd tell you to sit and watch them work for a while, but that's how a guy gets a restraining order. Regardless, you can take how they operate and glean useful advice from them. You can do that from anyone—and the fact that you're reading this is evidence that you're looking for ways to do that. That means you've taken steps towards being a sales dynamo. I'm excited to see what you will do.

Chapter Twelve: Cash Flow

I want to recap the dollars and cents of it all. (There's a dollar and sense pun in here that I'm resisting with great effort.) I know I've scattered a lot of those details through the book, but with nonfiction I like to compartmentalize data so that big ticket ideas can be easily located.

When I wrote about tech items and your Point of Sale, I mentioned things such as taxes, which can be (and should be) automatically added to every transaction. Our government makes every businessperson into an enforcer. As a libertarian, I disagree with the notion of taxes. I cannot fathom the ethics of being required to pay taxes on wages, then paying a tax to purchase items, then paying income tax on the sum of wages you collected annually, and then taxes again on property you already own. And just when you think you can escape taxes by dying, you learn there's a death tax too … and if you refuse to pay taxes, you go to prison under the enforcement of people with guns who are directed by those who made up these rules and very often pay none of these taxes. *That doesn't sound like a mafia protection scam at all.* At the risk of inciting an argument about roads and borders, I say all this to note that even as violently and morally opposed as I am to taxes, I collect them and pay them. You can (and should) change people's hearts and minds, convince them of your ideals, and work to make change, but do that from behind your pen and paper. It's pretty hard to sell books from behind bars.

At the end of this section, I will lay out a few profit-and-loss examples to help you see some of the math in action.

I'll point out areas where you can maximize your income from an event, and also point out some of the biggest ways to directly sink your boat and other places where many authors leak money.

Ways to increase total profit

Tracking data and using that to refine your presence at shows you return to

Selling omnibus editions

Making multiple sales

Having additional, trained help at your table who can replicate your sales tactics

Making smart choices that reduce risk

Using a fuel saving/coupon app

Bring your own food

Split hotel or other expenses

Find a gas miser vehicle (I bought a high mileage Prius for under $3,000 to use as my convention car. It doesn't fit much beyond my needs, but it paid for itself in the first year)

Be sure to take multiple forms of currency

Work your way into being a guest rather than a vendor (where the event pays your expenses)

Ways to lose money

Absorbing the tax burden of others (not charging sales tax)

Paying sales tax on your re-sale product

Failing to account for sales tax entirely

Overextending your product to bookstores and getting killed on returns

Running out of books on hand that you might otherwise sell

Getting a parking or speeding ticket

Not taking credit cards

Spending money on useless things

Forgetting important items

Acting like an event attendee rather than a vendor

There are a few other ways you can boost your presence and, ideally, your sales while at live shows. Some of the non-convention style shows revolve around these.

- Be a speaker or panelist
- Teach a workshop or class
- Utilize advertising and/or social media
- Harness relevant hashtags for an audience

As promised, here is the math on a few shows of different tiers. This assumes that you have a stock of books on hand. I generally keep 15-30 copies of any given title in stock and replace them as my stores deplete, so I'll only track the expense of the actual books sold. These are all shows I have done in the post-COVID era, and keep in mind that sales seem to be down 20-40% as we recover. I'll also post a few shows from before COVID. These are numbers that are typical (they are examples rather than exceptions) of experiences when using the techniques in this book. My numbers are rounded for simplicity's sake.

Example 1:
Tier 2
Pre-COVID
Number sold: 185
Days: 3
Cost of Fuel/lodging: 30   Cost of Food: 45   Cost of Product: 925
Fees: 180   Other Expenses: 20
Total loss: 1,200
Total income: 2,960
Net P/L: +$1,760
(Stayed with friends to avoid hotel costs)

Example 2:
Tier 4
Pre-COVID
Number sold: 61
Days: 3
Cost of Fuel/lodging: 30   Cost of Food: 32   Cost of Product: 305
Fees: 100   Other Expenses:
Total loss: 467
Total income: 915
Net P/L: +$448
(Stayed with friends to avoid hotel costs)

Example 3:
Tier 3B
Post-COVID
Number sold: 72
Days: 2
Cost of Fuel/lodging: 31   Cost of Food: 40   Cost   of Product: 360
Fees: 40   Other Expenses: 10

Total loss: 481
Total income: 935
Net P/L: +$454
(Stayed with friends to avoid hotel costs)

Example 4:
Tier 2
Post-COVID
Number sold: 165
Days: 3
Cost of Fuel/lodging: 315   Cost of Food: 40   Cost of Product: 825
Fees: 250   Other Expenses: 45
Total loss: 1,475
Total income: 2,145
Net P/L: +$670

Example 5:
Tier 3B
Post-COVID
Number sold: 38
Days: 1
Cost of Fuel/lodging: 30   Cost of Food: 14   Cost of Product: 165
Fees: 50   Other Expenses:
Total loss: 259
Total income: 546
Net P/L: +$287
(One-day show w/no hotel costs)

Example 6:
Tier 3A
Post-COVID
Number sold: 120

Days: 3
Cost of Fuel/lodging: 163   Cost of Food: 72   Cost of Product: 600
Fees: 150   Other Expenses:
Total loss: 985
Total income: 2,030
Net P/L: +$1,045

Example 7:
Tier 3A
Post-COVID
Number sold: 110
Days: 3
Cost of Fuel/lodging: 30   Cost of Food: 41   Cost of Product: 360
Fees: 0   Other Expenses:
Total loss: 431
Total income: 1,600
Net P/L: +$1,169
(Had guest status, no table or hotel costs)

Example 8:
Tier 3A
Post-COVID
Number sold: 59
Days: 2
Cost of Fuel/lodging: 119   Cost of Food: 12   Cost of Product: 280
Fees: 70   Other Expenses:
Total loss: 481
Total income: 858
Net P/L: +$377

Example 9:
Tier 1
Post-COVID
Number sold: 254
Days: 4
Cost of Fuel/lodging: 80   Cost of Food: 200   Cost of Product: 1270
Fees: 330   Other Expenses: 90
Total loss: 1970
Total income: 3710
Net P/L: +$1740
(Stayed with friends to avoid hotel costs)

Example 10:
Tier 2 (but under 10,000 people)
Post-COVID
Number sold: 133
Days: 2
Cost of Fuel/lodging: 135   Cost of Food: 75   Cost of Product: 665
Fees: 260   Other Expenses: 0
Total loss: 1,135
Total income: 2,114
Net P/L: +$979
(Stayed with friends to avoid hotel costs)

Cash Flow Breakdown

I wanted to give you a slice of the pre-con shows as well as the current state, which I expect to improve. You might notice there is not a lot of deviation pre/post COVID, but in the off-year, I spent a great deal of time tweaking and refining. I improved some books and some of my marketing materials at that time, so my numbers didn't see a noticeable dip because of the changes I made. It is noticeable, at least to me, because I pay attention to my numbers.

The biggest factor in making profit is keeping down your expenses, especially lodging. If I have a friend nearby or can otherwise secure free lodging, I am three times more likely to do a show in that area.

I intentionally included a spread of different types of shows but didn't use any Tier 1 data. It is mostly similar to what I have already, from a profit/loss standpoint, with the exception that it is a lot more work. This year I am scheduled for 33 weekend dates, so we'll extrapolate some data based on the spread we have here.

Average income over eight shows: a little above $775. It's about $26,000 *net profit* over the course of a year. That doesn't include things like on-line sales and other sources of book revenue such as consulting and author services that I provide. (Contact me directly with interest in that.) Extrapolating data from just eight shows is a stretch, however, and I think my actual potential this year is more like $35,000, which is somewhere between three and four thousand copies (and that's with taking off most of January-May this year, with only three shows over those four months, and two of them being smaller Tier 3 events).

The more data you have, the easier it is to see trends. As you can tell from the bottom line P/L and other notes, the smaller shows can wind up being huge financial losses if the expenses aren't mitigated, and the way I keep my profit margins at acceptable levels is by being savvy with travel costs: compare examples #2 and #4. I sold an extra 100 books and made more than double gross income only to make about $220 after the expenses were paid. Sometimes you work your rear end off for only little gains. When you see those trends, you can ask yourself, "How much is the expended energy worth?" The smaller shows are less sexy, but you can find a groove in them that is actually more profitable in the short term, though the larger shows can end up also growing your platform and translating to some long-term success.

Make sure you have enough data to work with before you make radical choices or try to reinvent the wheel. You should, preferably, have more than a year's worth of data first. And your data should show steady improvements in your skills and your numbers will also increase because of repeat customers... I know I previously said, "Nobody is coming to the show to see you," but after a year or two, that can become untrue. I've had some people return to shows in later years looking for me and planning to buy the next installments.

This business is about building and continuing to grow on the foundation of your backlist. It's good to remember what you're built on, what motivates you to get to the next level, and to remember that *this is a business* ... and you need to treat it accordingly.

Chapter Thirteen: Wrap Up

Good, Bad, and Ugly

As we wrap up, let's talk about the good, the bad, and the ugly. I like that as a chapter theme, and I've got that western whistle music stuck in my head now. You know it: woo-oo-oo woo-oh wah wah wah.

The ugly

I'm going to give you an honest truth. Sometimes when I talk with a new author contact who I've met at a booth and they ask me what I think, I lie. Remember when I said that you had to give *explicit* permission?

Story time. I have many friends who entertain global travelers, whether it be missions work or international students or faculty at higher ed. There are always cultural issues at play when we communicate—but when we're a member of that culture, we don't notice them. When we cross cultures, those cultural blind spots come across loud and clear. In one such instance, a girl who really wanted to go to an American's home for supper was asked,

"Would you like to come eat?" She said *no*. "You're sure you don't want to?" She said *no, thank you*. And then the Americans walked away, and the international student felt bad thinking they did not really want to invite her. In their culture, it is understood that you must ask three times if you really want them there; the first two invites are formality and surface-level politeness. Kind of like, "Go tell your sister you are sorry." It has no real meaning beyond lip service.

When an author says, "I'd love to know your thoughts," I go into polite mode. I'm quite certain that, "Yes, please be honest with your thoughts," actually means, "Please tell me that you love it and I'm sure I must be one lucky break away from the bestsellers list." Unless that person convinces me to give them my dead level best, I operate overall on "only say culturally polite things," but not because I want to be bound up in that culture of insincerity—I really want to give feedback—but because if you don't actually want it, it's going to feel like a cruel sucker-punch. It's not a sucker punch, nor is it cruel, but there is pain in it, much like weightlifting. No pain, no gain.

Not only have I seen authors with this mindset, but I know it's the default mindset because I, too, suffered from it early on. I didn't like hearing criticism and wrote off critical comments while grumping something about judging books on covers or some other such nonsense. Meanwhile, through writing short fiction for a few years and working with a critique group, I got very good at learning to take criticism for what it is: a set of honest eyes which I can use to refine my book and improve it.

Of course, my next thought was *now if someone judges my book by its cover, they'll miss out on a great story!* I realized that, if I want my stories to be read, the onus was on me to get a good cover. DIY covers often indicate a lack of quality or incoherent editing. I used to have a review policy on my blog and many writers were butt hurt, but janky covers usually indicate janky stories.

For my reviews, I asked to be queried like any other media source. I still keep one of those queries as an example of what *not* to do. The purple prose was so over the top that I imagine the writer walks around in a top hat and monocle, speaking with a voice that drips with condescension.

Purple prose (or high falutin' talk, as my grandmammy says it), obfuscates the true meaning—like when an author uses obfuscates instead of just saying *hides.* Readers can't tell what the heck you're saying when using "purple prose" because the fancy talk gets in the way of understanding. If you were alive in the 1990s and remember the one where (that's a Friends reference for all you kids), Joey learned about the thesaurus feature on Chandler's laptop. He changed every word to something else to try to make himself sound smart/fancy. The result was incomprehensible.

Don't be like Joey. Talk normally. Be understood. Get your point across. And don't deny your audience access to your book by putting a bad cover on it. At some point, it is *on you* and not on them to get this done.

Covers are the number one tool in your sales toolbox. Number two is the blurb; if it doesn't hook the reader, they will lose interest quickly. You are at a live event and many people arevying for a piece of the pie. If your cover and blurb are subpar, then your bells and whistles are not loud enough, compared to others, to garner the needed attention. Use that knowledge and refine. Refine, refine, refine. Knowing where to refine is knowledge only gained by seeking that genuine criticism/feedback.

Refine? But also, let your work "be" at some point too. At some point, you must accept that the book will have to simply be what it is. It will never please everybody. And that's fine.

I gave an author a free consultation on her back cover blurb. She was floundering and frustrated. I told her to give me the main elements and plot of her book and, like many newer authors, she rambled aimlessly for a long time, trying to stuff in every subplot and detail. Subplot elements are for the story, not the blurb. You must be able to strip out all the neat parts and let the reader discover them while you focus on a sharp enough hook to grab them and move the person to the POS, click Buy, etc. I rewrote her blurb. Short (about 300 words). Succinct. Powerful. Tight. "I haven't been excited about the book until seeing this blurb. *I want to read this.* It's perfect." I told her to sit on it for a few days and then re-read and tweak it if need be.

A few days later, I saw her back on the critique group we both share and she's on her sixth revision since me with a 900 word, conflated and confusing, unexciting back cover summary that tries again to hit on every subplot and describe every character. Other "helpers" contributed: what about X, you should give us more about Y, other authors talk about Z, I don't write the genre, but you *need* ABC.

Here's the point—Don't listen to every voice. They'll disagree. Just find what is going to work, and then drill down on *what will work best.* Coincidentally, all those issues the other authors (most of whom weren't even familiar with her genre), asked questions answered by the book. A potential reader/buyer (as opposed to an armchair copywriter) will buy the book *to answer those questions.* If the book is on target for the genre and sets the hook properly, answering those questions is counterproductive. This writer was excited because the hook was written for the perfect target market: her. *Write for that market, not your aunt Ethel—* neither King nor Rowling could write a blurb that'll make Aunt Ethel buy a book she's already set against.

It's okay to leave a reader wanting more. That makes them buy the book (and more if you have a series). It's more an attitude than a practical skill but become fine with the fact that your book isn't going to hook everyone. And a top-heavy blurb hooks hardly anyone. Those overloaded summary blurbs have been a mainstay of traditional publishing for a century. But your back cover needs to *work.* It needs to sell books. This is an area where indies have beaten the ever-living-crud out of trade presses. Even the Big 5 still often write those kinds of blurbs. But they've learned that tight and cleverly barbed hooks are partly what lured readers away from their products, or at least helped establish the validity of independents and knocked the gatekeepers down a peg.

I guess what I'm trying to say is that *the ugly* is often defined as authors cutting corners and hoping everybody overlooks that fact. The Ugly truth is that, very often, the reason your product doesn't sell is that it's not a good product. That is usually the case when a book is released too early and/or without the proper professionals involved (cover artists and editors).

The bad

Let's talk about other things that can go wrong for your author business but that aren't directly related to your book as a product. Sometimes you have less control over *the bad* things but, ultimately, you are still the one on the hook for them, and for all aspects of your live book events.

Evaluation. Should you be at this show? If the event's target audience is a church crowd, it probably won't work for your open-door-sex Erotica series. If it's a booth at the Republican National Convention, your Anti-Trump hit piece is going to villainize you and tank your sales. Likewise with a take-down of Obama at the DNC.

If your sales have been below expectations, you might look first at the kind of audience you are entertaining and how it relates to your book and genre. It might be as simple as following trends. (For a period, Vampire PNR was the hottest thing on the market, and then it slumped after everyone and their dog started writing it— probably not because of over-saturation [as a genre, the romance market is almost impossible to over-saturate], but because of reader fatigue on the sub-genre.)

Book signings, or events at bookstores, defy norms, however. At bookstore signings, you are at the mercy of whoever walks through the door on any given day. Customers could be anywhere on the spectrum of genre fandoms. I do mostly comic convention events because it neatly aligns with the likes and desires of my market. But I regularly see crime and thriller writers there, and also paranormal romance. While authors in both of those markets do make sales, they will have stronger sales at niche events. A romance book fair will probably see higher sales for the latter and there are other events a crime novel would perform better at, although they do sell adequately in most markets. I am not saying don't try to sell outside your perfect market—sometimes you just need to do an event. But you may lower the ceiling on your expectations somewhat for an event outside your ideal genre; you should be aware that it can impact your total sales numbers.

Pitch. Let's talk about a sales hook. It is possible to have a hook that works well for one event that flops at the next. It's perfectly acceptable to alter it based on your audience. Let's look at my Dekker's Dozen science fiction series, for example. If I am at a sci-fi con or a general comic con, I'll identify people who might be dressed like characters from the Firefly television show, which many of my early readers compared it to. I pitch it as the next best thing to Firefly. If they haven't seen the beloved series, I'll use "The Magnificent Seven in space," or "It has The Mandalorian vibes," as a comparison. But if the audience is an anime crowd, I will use a comparison to Cowboy Bebop or Outlaw Star.

I mentioned it above, but there is something to be said for not overloading your audience with a twenty-minute overview of the book. Use your pitch to identify and pique interest, and then lead into a soft ask. If your cover and blurb are on point and the story fits the market for the present audience, you should sell well. If not, you might wonder why/how you're failing to engage them. Maybe it's the excitement level (or lack of it) in your voice ... maybe its other factors. But you can always ask a friend if you can pitch him or her and have them provide feedback on what would make them more likely to buy. If you're brave enough, you could even ask a random potential buyer and explain that you're looking for feedback to improve your sales skills. "What can I do or say that would make my book irresistible to someone like you?" They'll likely tell you.

Bottom-line Summary. I've done shows where I have felt like I was on fire all weekend, and then I'll do a recap of my sales and expenses and realize that the show was not nearly as profitable as I'd thought. This happens especially when expenses tip the scale. Even with strong sales, it can be difficult to post a profit if you get a speeding ticket(s), have to pay for a tow truck, or a hotel double booking error or a snowstorm forces you to pay for an unexpected, upgraded room or move to a different venue (all things that have happened to me over the years).

The bigger the shows that you do, and the further you travel for them, will create more opportunities for sneaky little expenses to creep in. Mileage, parking, food, and lodging are black holes that can eat as much money as you give them. Look back at Example 8 in the cash flow examples I provided in the last chapter; the show was a fairly small one that was a pretty far drive, but 59 books were still more than double the numbers of the three other authors who were present. I was honestly shooting for 75. I kept my food and other costs way down on this spring show but stayed in a $50 per night hotel. You can see that I had to spend more than a dollar per book sold in fuel costs—that was partly due to the high cost of fuel, which had increased by nearly a dollar per gallon since the last show I'd traveled to in late winter. It was disappointing to see so many dollars get burned up—even with my Prius; and with me writing this in mid-2022, where fuel prices reached a new all-time high, the experts have claimed that this is part of our new normal and should be considered when you look at your budget. That show was on the line between a Tier 1 and 2 (mainly because of how COVID impacted attendance numbers) and I netted about $650 in profit. I wince to look at how I paid nearly $100 to park—something I don't normally take into account except when vending in downtown city areas. Still, it was a pretty great show, and I got seated next to Tom Cook, who drew a lot of my favorite childhood animated shows, such as Masters of the Universe and Scooby Doo. (Plus, he swapped a couple of autographed prints for one of my books, which was cool. A lot of booth neighbors will do similar things.) But you can't pay your college loans with awesome autographs and sketches of Pickle Rick. What would have been better than being seated next to a great booth neighbor would have been selling another fifty books, which would have gotten me closer to my expectations for that show.

Expectations. Bad expectations can also be a huge factor in why your books don't sell well. Maybe they are selling as well as they can in the given circumstances. We can't predict things like the sales fall-out and public hysteria that we suffered under pandemic protocols. Luckily, I understand that this is a marathon business and not a sprint, so I've swallowed the lumps and upped my writing game. *Nothing sells books 1 & 2 like book 3.*

The things we've endured these last couple of years have been unpredictable. But we can control our expectations and our own ability to pivot and cultivate ingenuity. We can refuse to build unrealistic ideas for our sales numbers. That will keep us from frustration. Give a new show, or a show during strange circumstances, a cautious approach and have the mentality that you are there to gather data. You'll need to do your best, just so you can measure your results against an honest attempt to sell well—that alone should be your standard metric.

The good

What about when everything goes *right?*

Sometimes, everything just clicks. You hit new sales numbers. Some B or C-list celebrity loves your stuff and talks about it on his or her social media. Some random human buys your supper.

We've talked a lot about what it looks like when things go wrong, but let's talk about what *could* happen at some show. Let's build a hypothetical situation just for the sake of the dream.

What if:

The show is a large show and within easy driving distance so you can sleep in your own bed at night and even bring your spouse or a good friend to help you sell—and make the booth time run at peak-fun. That's right, no lodging costs, and you brought your own lunch in a cooler.

You nail the sales side and hit a new high mark. For Tier 1 and 2 shows, I am typically aiming at 300 book sales, so let's say it's a touch higher at 350 (though I know 500 books is doable at these large shows).

At night, your favorite B-list celebrity tweets a picture of you and him hanging out and getting drinks at an evening after-party. He's holding your book, and you get an extra $500 worth of unexpected online sales by the end of the convention from it, plus a bump in NL sign-ups from the added web traffic.

Given the costs I've tracked for shows this size, let's say the cost of entry was $300, which is on par for a show like that. Our income would be around $6,300 minus $300 for fees and gas is negligible due to the distance. Product cost is $1,750, but we should add the $500 profit from the online sales bump since we know it was due to the show. Net, you're profiting almost $5,000 from this one event.

Obviously, this should not be your standard expectation, but it's a very realistic opportunity if everything were to hit just right. It can be an amazing high point of your yearly sales schedule. Your regular expectations are more likely to hit the $400-700 mark and have the occasional $1,300-1,500 profit from larger shows where you're hitting the 120-book sales mark, give or take a few books.

You won't hit those numbers out of the gate. You'll need a few books to have the variety and/or an amazing table presence with quality materials and art. That means that, even early in a writing career, if you work it you can average $800 in net profit per show or more. If you do half the weekends out of the year and average around $800, you'll earn about $21,000 and continue to scale up from there. That means you can add those sales figures to your audiobook and ebook sales and other avenues of revenue, making this a very viable path to hitting the kinds of numbers you need to make this your full-time career, even with a less than perfect online presence.

Does this feel like the end?

There's actually more!

In the table of contents I promised a bonus chapter covering pricing hacks. That bonus chapter is being offered as a free resource and is available at this exclusive web link:

www.authorchristopherdschmitz.com/authorservices

Here you can also find online content, videos, digital courses, freebies, and workshops. You can also get info about author mentoring, and a link to an online community.

About the author:

Christopher D. Schmitz is an indie author from the fly-over states who dabbles in game design. He has published award winning science fiction, fantasy, and humor. He's written and freelanced for a variety of outlets, including a blog that has helped countless writers on their publishing journey. On any given weekend, he can be found at pop culture and comic conventions across the USA or playing his bagpipes for people. You can look him up at
www.authorchristopherdschmitz.com.

Thanks for reading and sharing!

If you enjoyed it or find anything helpful within its pages won't you please take a moment to leave me a review at your favorite retailer? Sharing this title with your friends on social media and requesting it via your local library will also help immensely. Discoverability is the lifeblood of success for authors and we can't continue writing without help!

I also hope you will keep tabs on me by joining my mailing list. You can get free books and other updates by signing up for that list at: www.AuthorChristopherDSchmitz.com.

Christopher D Schmitz

Please Visit
http://www.authorchristopherdschmitz.com
Sign-up on the mailing list for exclusives and extras

other ways to connect with me:
Follow me on Twitter:
https://twitter.com/cylonbagpiper
Follow me on Goodreads:
www.goodreads.com/author/show/129258.Christopher Schmitz
Like/Follow me on Facebook:
https://www.facebook.com/authorchristopherdschmitz

Subscribe to my blog:
https://authorchristopherdschmitz.wordpress.com
Favorite me at Smashwords:
www.smashwords.com/profile/view/authorchristopherdschmitz
My Amazon Author Profile:
amazon.com/author/christopherdschmitz
Follow me at Bookbub:
www.bookbub.com/authors/christopher-d-schmitz

Christopher D. Schmitz